A DASH OF SZECHWAN

A DASH OF SZECHWAN

BY CHEN KENTARO

Published on behalf of Meritus International by Marshall Cavendish Cuisine,
an imprint of Marshall Cavendish International (Asia)

A member of the
Times Publishing Group

National Library Board, Singapore Cataloguing in Publication Data

Name(s): Chen, Kentaro.
Title: A dash of Szechwan / by Chen Kentaro.
Description: Second edition. | Singapore : Marshall Cavendish Cuisine, 2018.
Identifier(s): OCN 1048617387 | ISBN 978-981-47-9482-4 (paperback)
Subject(s): LCSH: Cooking, Chinese--Sichuan style. | Cooking, Chinese.
Classification: DDC 641.595138--dc23

Photographer: Hongde Photography

Printed in Singapore

I am blessed with extraordinary people in my life
whose guidance, encouragement, and support
enrich my journey beyond words:

my family,
who are my true inspiration
for all that I am and all that I do;

my amazing friends and colleagues,
at Shisen Hanten and
Mandarin Orchard Singapore;

Chef Yuki Sugaya,
who has had my back from the first day we met as
Shisen Hanten chefs in training all those years ago.

guests and diners,
who continue to embrace
Shisen Hanten by Chen Kentaro
with their esteemed patronage

—my immense love and gratitude to you all.
This book is for you.

My very special thanks to Shigeru Akashi and
Dr. Stephen Riady of OUE Limited,
and to each and every one
that helped make this book possible.

To Dad and Grandpa
—I can only hope I make you proud.

Contents

Foreword

Long before Chen Kentaro became the celebrated chef that he is, I first knew him as a young, bright-eyed boy who liked to follow his father around.

This was in the 1990s when Fuji Television's long-running cooking reality series, *Iron Chef*, was at the height of its popularity. On the show, I battled it out in the French cuisine category while Kentaro's father, Chen Kenichi, made his mark competing in the Chinese cuisine category.

Behind the scenes and beyond the fame, the show yielded for us, competing chefs, friendships that have endured over the years. It is through the bond Kenichi and I share that I have had a front row seat to his son's remarkable journey into becoming the culinary force that he is today.

Kentaro coming into his own is no mean feat. After all, he carries with him a legacy that was passed down by his father and his grandfather—both icons recognised for their contribution to the growth of Szechwan cuisine in Japan through the establishment of the Shisen Hanten chain.

While it stood to reason that Kentaro would choose to follow in the footsteps of his forebears, eyes were also on him to step out from under their shadows. And so it was that a determined and charismatic Kentaro went about carving a niche for himself—and what a niche it is turning out to be! A Michelin-rated restaurant, no less, to add to the many feathers in his cap.

In the course of knowing him and working alongside each other on many occasions, I have come to admire the energy of his youth, the idealism of his dreams, and the heart behind the talent. I recognise Kentaro's thoughtful, affable personality as he celebrates his Szechwan lineage in the pages of this cookbook.

Most of the recipes start off with little personal stories, with stunning food photography and useful visuals that demonstrate the step-by-step preparation of more complex techniques. He carefully and very generously selected each of the recipes to share, no doubt in the hope of taking you through a discovery of the fascinating diversity of Szechwan cuisine.

More than a cookbook, this is a labour of love that is unmistakably Kentaro's.

Hiroyuki Sakai
March 2018

Chef Hiroyuki Sakai is the longest-reigning Iron Chef French. He was bestowed Chevalier de l'Ordre du Mérite Agricole by the French Republic in 2005, and in 2009 received the Gendai No Meikou, a prestigious national award honouring Japan's foremost artisans in various fields.

Introduction

For as long as I can remember, I was surrounded by chefs in my family. Despite the gap between generations, food has always been the common thread that bound us. While some may say it was inevitable that I pursued the same career as my father and grandfather, it was a decision I made for myself very early on.

I knew for sure I would make it my mission to carry on the family legacy. To say that I looked up to them both is an understatement, because they personified in every way the kind of chef and mentor I aspired to be.

In my pursuit to specialise in Szechwan cuisine, I trained and worked in various Szechwan restaurants across Chengdu, the capital of China's Szechwan province. I am blessed to have had Szechwan master chefs, including my father, as mentors. Not only did they help me perfect my cooking techniques, but they also instilled in me the discipline and entrepreneurship I needed for the role I would eventually play at Shisen Hanten.

2014 marked a milestone for me and for the Shisen Hanten brand with the opening of Shisen Hanten by Chen Kentaro at the iconic Mandarin Orchard Singapore. I was feeling the pressure, so I had to keep reminding myself to focus on what I set out to do first and foremost—to promote a greater appreciation for Szechwan flavours among audiences in Singapore through my family's signature recipes.

Two years later, the restaurant was awarded two stars in the Michelin Guide Singapore 2016, and then again in 2017. No one was prouder than my father, and I could not have been happier to share the achievement with him and everyone who has been with me through every step.

In this, the first ever English translation of some of my recipes as well as time-honoured recipes of the Chen family, I take the opportunity to share with more people my love of Szechwan cooking. The book features 50 recipes, including Shisen Hanten signatures, across six categories. You will also find recipes for hearty stocks and traditional Szechwan sauces, marinades, and seasonings that you can use for a great variety of dishes.

I cannot wait for you to try your hand at these recipes and enjoy them with family and friends.

Chen Kentaro

Appetisers & Dim Sum

前菜与点心

1. Use a blow torch to remove any bubbles on the surface of the egg mixture.

2. Place the bowls in a steamer and steam for 8–10 minutes until the mixture is set.

3. Ladle the crab roe soup over the steamed foie gras chawanmushi.

Foie Gras Chawanmushi with Crab Roe Soup 蟹黄鹅肝汤

SERVES	4
PREPARATION TIME	30 minutes
COOKING TIME	30 minutes

INGREDIENTS

FOIE GRAS CHAWANMUSHI

40 g	foie gras
1	egg

SEASONING

200 ml	chicken stock (page 139)
1 tsp	Shaoxing rice wine
½ tsp	oyster sauce
1 pinch	salt
1 dash	ground white pepper

CRAB ROE SOUP

1 tsp	shallot oil
40 g	crabmeat, shredded
10 g	crab roe
20 g	boiled bamboo shoot, finely sliced
30 g	carrot, puréed
300 ml	chicken stock (page 139)
100 ml	pork stock (page 139)
1 pinch	salt
1 dash	ground white pepper
½ tsp	sugar
1 tsp	chicken seasoning powder
½ Tbsp	Shaoxing rice wine
½ tsp	Japanese soy sauce
1 tsp	oyster sauce
2 Tbsp	potato starch, mixed with a little water into a paste
1 tsp	chicken oil (page 139)
1 tsp	palm oil

Out of all my father's creations during his *Iron Chef* days, this dish stood out the most to me for its simplicity and bold flavours. When we were planning to open Shisen Hanten by Chen Kentaro in Singapore, I knew I had to include this dish on the menu. With a few tweaks, it quickly grew to become a signature in the restaurant.

METHOD

1. Prepare the foie gras *chawanmushi*. Combine the ingredients for the seasoning in a pot and bring to a boil. Remove from the heat and set aside to cool.

2. Place the foie gras, egg, and cooled seasoning into a food processor and blend well. Pass the egg mixture through a sieve and divide among 4 heatproof bowls.

3. Use a blow torch to remove any bubbles on the surface of the egg mixture, then cover the bowls with cling wrap.

4. Place the bowls in a steamer and steam for 8–10 minutes until the mixture is set.

5. Prepare the crab roe soup. Heat the shallot oil in a wok over medium heat. Lightly sauté all the remaining ingredients except for the potato starch paste, chicken oil, and palm oil. Bring the mixture to a simmer, then add the potato starch paste and stir to thicken the sauce. Add the chicken oil and palm oil and mix quickly.

6. Ladle the crab roe soup over the steamed foie gras *chawanmushi* and serve.

蟹黄鹅肝汤

SERVES 3–4
PREPARATION TIME 40 minutes
COOKING TIME 20 minutes

Steamed Chicken with Mala Sauce

口
水
鸡

INGREDIENTS

1	chicken breast
1	chicken thigh
1	Japanese eggplant
50 g	soy bean sprouts

MALA SAUCE

100 ml	water
200 g	sugar
100 ml	sweet soy sauce
225 ml	Zhenjiang vinegar
225 ml	Japanese soy sauce
150 ml	chilli oil
150 ml	*lao you*
1 dash	Szechwan pepper oil
1 pinch	red Szechwan peppercorn powder

GARNISHING

1 Tbsp	crushed peanuts
1 tsp	roasted white sesame seeds
2–3 sprigs	coriander leaves

*L*ao you is an ingredient commonly used in Szechwan cuisine. It is a type of chilli oil distinctly vibrant in colour and flavour from having been processed with various spices such as Szechwan peppercorns, garlic, and ginger. I find that using *lao you* as a dressing for the tender chicken slices adds depth to the mouth-watering flavour of this cold appetiser.

METHOD

1. Place the chicken breast and thigh in a steamer and steam for 8–10 minutes or until the juices run clear when the meat is pierced with a skewer. Set aside to cool.

2. Combine the ingredients for the *mala* sauce in a bowl and mix well. Measure out 200 ml for use in this recipe. Refrigerate until cold. The excess *mala* sauce can be kept in an airtight container and stored in the refrigerator for up to 1 week.

3. Peel the eggplant and cut into 7–8-cm lengths. Place in a steamer and steam for 8 minutes. Set aside to cool.

4. Arrange the cooled eggplant and soy bean sprouts on a serving plate. Cut the steamed chicken into bite-sized pieces and arrange on the eggplant and soy bean sprouts.

5. Drizzle the *mala* sauce over the steamed chicken. Garnish with crushed peanuts, roasted white sesame seeds, and coriander leaves. Serve the remaining *mala* sauce on the side.

Mixed Salad with Mala Dressing

乱鸡八杂

SERVES	3–4
PREPARATION TIME	2 hours
COOKING TIME	30 minutes

In our restaurants in Japan, we take turns to prepare meals for the staff each day. Chefs use food from the night before to make breakfast. One day, a chef improvised by chopping up various ingredients and mixing it with *mala* sauce. Everyone loved the salad so much that we decided to include it on the restaurant menu. In Japan, we have this saying "luck exists in the leftovers"—so eat up!

INGREDIENTS

1 litre	chicken stock (page 139)
1 litre	water
50 g	abalone
50 g	chicken, deboned
50 g	pig's tongue
50 g	pig's ear
50 g	celery, cut into 1-cm cubes
1	Japanese cucumber, cut into 1-cm cubes
As needed	salt
10 g	Japanese leek, white part
3–4 slices	ginger, peeled
50 g	roast ham, cut into 1-cm cubes
50 g	jellyfish, rinsed to remove excess salt and cut into small pieces
1	century egg, peeled and cut into 1-cm cubes
4	cherry tomatoes, cut into 1-cm cubes
½ Tbsp	chilli oil
½ tsp	Szechwan pepper oil
1 pinch	red Szechwan peppercorn powder

SEASONING

2 Tbsp	Japanese soy sauce
1½ Tbsp	sake
2 tsp	sugar
1 tsp	sweet soy sauce (*tianjiangyou*)
1 Tbsp	chilli oil

METHOD

1. Combine the chicken stock and water in a pot. Bring to a boil. Add the abalone and chicken, and boil until the chicken is done. Drain and cut the abalone and chicken into 1-cm cubes.

2. Add the pig's tongue and ears to the boiling stock, and cook until tender. Drain and cut the tongue and ears into 1-cm cubes.

3. Place the celery and cucumber cubes in a bowl and sprinkle with a large pinch of salt. Let sit for a few minutes to draw out excess moisture. Drain well.

4. Cut the Japanese leek in half lengthwise, then cut into 1-cm slices. Slice the ginger into 1-cm squares.

5. Place the abalone, chicken, pig's tongue, pig's ears, celery, cucumber, Japanese leek, and ginger in a bowl. Add the roast ham, jellyfish, century egg, tomatoes, and seasoning, and mix well.

6. Drizzle with the chilli oil and Szechwan pepper oil, and top with a sprinkle of red Szechwan peppercorn powder. Serve.

SERVES	3–4
PREPARATION TIME	2 hours
COOKING TIME	30 minutes

Sliced Beef, Beef Tongue and Tripe with Mala Sauce

夫妻肺片

INGREDIENTS

1.5 litres	chicken stock (page 139)
100 g	beef shank
1 dash	Shaoxing rice wine
1 pinch	salt
20 g	beef tongue
100 g	beef tripe
1 tsp	sesame oil
30 g	carrot
½	Japanese cucumber

SEASONING

½ tsp	grated garlic
1 tsp	sweet bean paste (*tianmianjiang*)
1 tsp	sesame oil
½ tsp	sugar
½ tsp	Japanese rice vinegar
½ Tbsp	Japanese soy sauce
½ Tbsp	chilli oil
3–4	red Szechwan peppercorns

The Chinese name for this popular Szechwan appetiser literally translates to "husband and wife lung slices". It is said to have been created by a couple from Chengdu, the capital of Szechwan province, who sold offal cooked in spices. I like this dish because it incorporates various ingredients to create a unique texture.

METHOD

1. Bring the chicken stock to a boil in a pot. Add the beef shank and cook for a few minutes, then remove and set aside. Add the rice wine and salt to the stock, then return the beef shank to the pot. Let the beef cool in the stock before removing and cutting into thin slices.

2. Boil a pot of water and parboil the beef tongue and tripe. Remove and cut into thin slices.

3. Bring a fresh pot of water to a boil and add the sliced beef, beef tongue and tripe. Reduce to a light boil, then drain and season with a pinch of salt and sesame oil.

4. Peel the carrot and cucumber, then make decorative slits on the sides before cutting into thin slices.

5. Place the carrot and cucumber slices in a bowl with the sliced beef, beef tongue and tripe. Add the seasoning and mix well. Serve.

Vegetarian Yuba-maki

素腐皮卷

SERVES	3–4
PREPARATION TIME	20 minutes
COOKING TIME	10 minutes

INGREDIENTS

30 g	carrot, peeled
1	green capsicum
2	shiitake mushrooms
As needed	salt
100 g	bean sprouts
1 dash	sesame oil
3	dried *yuba* sheets (dried tofu skin)
3–4 Tbsp	cooking oil
2–3	green shiso leaves

MUSTARD SAUCE

1 tsp	mustard
1½ Tbsp	Japanese soy sauce
½ tsp	Japanese rice vinegar
¼ tsp	sugar
1 tsp	sesame oil

In Japan, these rolls are usually made using only bean sprouts. Here I have added other vegetables to create layer upon layer of flavours and textures. I find that this pairs well with sake.

METHOD

1. Slice the carrot, capsicum, and mushrooms into matchsticks.

2. Bring a pot of water to a boil and add a pinch of salt. Blanch the carrot, capsicum, mushrooms, and bean sprouts in the water until slightly wilted. Drain well and season with salt and sesame oil.

3. Combine the ingredients for the mustard sauce in a bowl. Set aside.

4. Wipe a *yuba* sheet with a moist kitchen towel and spread it out on a work surface. Place a third of the vegetable mixture on the *yuba* sheet and roll it up tightly to ensure that the rolls do not come apart when frying. Repeat with the remaining vegetable mixture.

5. Heat the cooking oil in a pan over medium heat. Gently lower the rolls into the hot oil and cook until the *yuba* skin is crispy. Remove and drain well.

6. Cut the rolls into bite-sized pieces, then arrange on a serving plate with shiso leaves. Drizzle with mustard sauce and serve.

1

Peel the eggplant and cut into 7–8-cm long sticks.

2

Roast the shishito peppers and green chillies in a dry pan.

3

Mince the roasted shishito peppers and green chillies.

4

Continue to mince until the mixture is pasty.

SERVES	3–4
PREPARATION TIME	10 minutes
COOKING TIME	40 minutes

Steamed Eggplant with Shishito Pepper and Green Chilli Paste

擂椒茄子

INGREDIENTS

250 g	Japanese eggplants
70 g	shishito peppers
40 g	green chillies
2	century eggs, peeled
1½ Tbsp	peanut oil
½ tsp	grated garlic

SEASONING

2 tsp	Japanese soy sauce
½ tsp	sugar
½ tsp	oyster sauce
2 tsp	chicken seasoning powder
½ tsp	Japanese rice vinegar
½ tsp	sesame oil

My version of the traditional green chilli paste incorporates shishito peppers and century eggs. While most people might find this combination unusual, I guarantee you will enjoy it once you've tried it.

METHOD

1. Peel the eggplants and cut into 7–8-cm long sticks. Place in a steamer and steam for 8 minutes. Set aside to cool.

2. In a dry pan over medium heat, roast the shishito peppers and green chillies until they are fragrant and slightly charred. Set aside to cool.

3. Mince the century eggs. Mince the roasted shishito peppers and green chillies.

4. Combine the minced century eggs with the minced shishito peppers and green chillies. Continue to mince until the mixture is pasty. Transfer to a bowl.

5. Heat the peanut oil over high heat until aromatic.

6. Add the heated peanut oil, grated garlic, and seasoning to the paste. Mix well.

7. Arrange the cooled eggplants on a serving plate and top with the paste. Serve.

擂椒茄子

SERVES	3–4
PREPARATION TIME	10 minutes
COOKING TIME	30 minutes

Capsicum and Century Egg with Fragrant Dressing

彩椒皮蛋

INGREDIENTS

3	century eggs, peeled
2	green capsicums
½	red capsicum
½	yellow capsicum
30 g	Japanese leek, white part
2-cm knob	ginger, peeled
3 g	facing heaven peppers

SEASONING

1 tsp	sugar
1 pinch	salt
1½ Tbsp	Japanese soy sauce
½ Tbsp	sesame oil

This vegetarian dish features *chao tian jiao*, cone-shaped chilli peppers otherwise known as facing heaven peppers, popularly used in Szechwan cuisine. When sautéed, the peppers will change in taste to add a smoky flavour and a punch of heat to any dish.

METHOD

1. Slice the century eggs. Cut the green, red, and yellow capsicums into bite-sized pieces. Cut the leek into 1-cm lengths. Slice the ginger thinly. Remove the seeds from the facing heaven peppers.

2. In a dry pan over medium heat, roast the facing heaven peppers until slightly charred. Remove from the heat and cut into fine slices.

3. Reheat the pan and roast the green, red, and yellow capsicums until fragrant and slightly charred. Transfer to a bowl.

4. Add the leek and ginger to the bowl.

5. Mix the seasoning and drizzle it over the ingredients in the bowl. Mix well.

6. Arrange the ingredients on a serving plate with the sliced century eggs and sprinkle with the sliced facing heaven peppers. Serve.

Fillet the ayu and reserve the bones.

Place a fillet on a wrapper and top with some fried bones.

Sandwich with another fillet, cut-side down.

Roll the wrapper up to enclose the fillets.

Ayu Spring Roll

香鱼春卷

SERVES	3–4
PREPARATION TIME	20 minutes
COOKING TIME	30 minutes

INGREDIENTS

4	*ayu* (sweetfish), each about 12-cm long
1 tsp	Shaoxing rice wine
1 pinch	salt
1 dash	ground white pepper
4	spring roll wrappers
2–3 Tbsp	plain flour, mixed with a little water into a paste
As needed	cooking oil
2–3	calamansi limes

SEASONING

⅓ tsp	chilli bean paste (*doubanjiang*)
⅓ tsp	grated ginger
1 dash	Shaoxing rice wine
½ tsp	oyster sauce

These *ayu* spring rolls are a great way to enjoy fish. They are crunchy and make a satisfying mid-day snack.

METHOD

1. Scale the fish and rinse. Cut off the head and trim the fins.

2. Remove the innards and place in a bowl. Add the seasoning and mix well. Refrigerate until needed.

3. Fillet the *ayu* and reserve the bones. Marinate the fillets with the rice wine, salt, and pepper. Set aside.

4. Heat some oil in a wok over medium heat. Add the fish bones and lower the heat. Fry until the bones are golden brown, then turn up the heat and fry until crispy.

5. Place the fillets cut-side up on a plate. Spread with the seasoned innards.

6. Place a fillet on one side of a spring roll sheet cut-side up. Top with some fried bones, then sandwich with another fillet, cut-side down. Spread some flour paste along the edges of the spring roll wrapper, then roll the wrapper up to enclose the fillets. Repeat with the remaining ingredients.

7. Heat sufficient oil for deep-frying in a wok. Lower the spring rolls into the hot oil and deep-fry until golden brown and crisp.

8. Drain well and serve with cut limes.

Boiled Szechwan Wonton with Spicy Sesame Sauce

钟
水
饺

SERVES	3–4
PREPARATION TIME	1½ hours
COOKING TIME	20 minutes

INGREDIENTS

WONTON SKIN

75 g	cake flour
75 g	bread flour
75–90 ml	boiling water

FILLING

2 g	Japanese leek, white part, chopped
2 slices	ginger, peeled
50 ml	water
100 g	minced pork
⅓ tsp	salt
1 dash	ground white pepper
1½ tsp	potato starch

SAUCE

5 Tbsp	sugar
3 Tbsp	Japanese soy sauce
1 Tbsp	superior soy sauce
1 Tbsp	*lao you*
2 Tbsp	chilli oil
⅓ Tbsp	Chinese sesame paste
1 pinch	toasted white sesame seeds

If you are a fan of spicy wontons, you are sure to love this rendition that uses spicy sesame sauce instead of the traditional chilli oil and soy sauce.

METHOD

1. Prepare the wonton skin. Place both types of flour in a bowl. Add the boiling water gradually, mixing until a dough is formed. Cover the bowl with cling wrap and set aside at room temperature for 30 minutes to 1 hour.

2. Knead the rested dough until smooth. Divide it into 20–25 equal pieces and roll out thinly using a rolling pin.

3. Prepare the filling. Place the Japanese leek, ginger, and water in a bowl. Squeeze the leek and ginger to extract the flavour, then strain the liquid and set aside. Knead the minced pork, then add the leek and ginger water, and mix well. Add the salt, pepper, and potato starch, and mix until combined.

4. Place a spoonful of the filling on a wonton skin and fold into a half-moon shape. Press the edges to seal. Repeat with the remaining ingredients.

5. Bring a pot of water to a boil and add the wontons. When the wontons float, remove with a slotted spoon. Place in a serving bowl.

6. Combine the ingredients for the sauce and mix well. Drizzle over the wontons and serve hot.

Soups, Vegetables & Tofu

Pork Belly and Daikon Soup

连锅汤

SERVES 8
PREPARATION TIME 20 minutes
COOKING TIME 30 minutes

INGREDIENTS

600 ml	chicken stock (page 139)
200 ml	pork stock (page 139)
150 g	pork belly
300 g	daikon, cut into rectangular slices
4–5	red Szechwan peppercorns
2–3	Japanese leeks, white part
4–5 slices	ginger, peeled
1 Tbsp	sake
1 pinch	salt
1 dash	ground white pepper

SEASONING

1½ Tbsp	chilli bean paste (*doubanjiang*)
2 Tbsp	Japanese soy sauce
1½ Tbsp	Japanese rice vinegar
1 Tbsp	chicken stock (page 139)
1 Tbsp	grated ginger
1 Tbsp	sesame oil
1 Tbsp	minced Japanese leek, white part

Contrary to popular belief, there are milder tasting soups in Szechwan cuisine beyond the classic hot and sour soup. Packed with nutrients and flavours, the pork belly and daikon soup is a simple yet remarkably tasty soup the whole family will enjoy.

METHOD

1. Combine both the stocks in a pot and bring to a boil. Add the pork, daikon, peppercorns, Japanese leek, and ginger, and boil for 20 minutes.

2. Remove the pork and cut into thin strips. Return the sliced pork to the pot. Season the stock with the sake, salt, and pepper.

3. Combine the ingredients for the seasoning in a bowl. Mix into the soup or serve on the side.

SERVES	3–4
PREPARATION TIME	10 minutes
COOKING TIME	20 minutes

Szechwan Hot and Sour Soup

四川酸辣汤

INGREDIENTS

15 g	lean pork
10 g	dried scallops, soaked to rehydrate
10 g	dried shiitake mushrooms, soaked to rehydrate
5 g	dried sea cucumber, soaked to rehydrate
5 g	boiled bamboo shoot
20 g	firm tofu
600 ml	chicken stock (page 139)
5 g	dried glass noodles, soaked to rehydrate
1 Tbsp	sake
1 pinch	salt
1½ Tbsp	Japanese soy sauce
1 tsp	ground white pepper
2 Tbsp	potato starch, mixed with a little water into a paste
1 Tbsp	beaten egg
1½ Tbsp	Japanese rice vinegar
1 dash	*lao you*

MARINADE

1 Tbsp	Shaoxing rice wine
1 pinch	salt
1 dash	ground white pepper
1 dash	Japanese soy sauce
1 Tbsp	beaten egg
1 Tbsp	potato starch
1 tsp	cooking oil

Our adaptation of this classic Szechwan dish is more savoury from the use of Japanese soy sauce. You can opt for Chinese soy sauce if you prefer a slightly sweeter taste. Always keep in mind to add the vinegar to the pot last, so as to preserve the aroma which will otherwise be lost through heating.

METHOD

1. Cut the pork into thin strips and marinate with the rice wine, salt, pepper, and soy sauce. Add the beaten egg and mix well. Add the potato starch and mix again. Add the oil and mix a third time. Set aside.

2. Shred the rehydrated dried scallops. Slice the mushrooms, sea cucumber, bamboo shoot, and firm tofu into strips.

3. Place chicken stock in a pot. Add the glass noodles, and the shredded and sliced ingredients, except for the tofu, and bring to a boil. Lower the heat and add the marinated pork, gently loosening it in the stock so it does not clump up.

4. Add the sake, salt, soy sauce, and pepper, followed by the tofu and stir.

5. Add the potato starch paste and simmer to thicken the soup.

6. Stir in the beaten egg and vinegar. Ladle into serving bowls and drizzle with *lao you*. Serve.

SERVES	8
PREPARATION TIME	20 minutes
COOKING TIME	4 hours

Steamed Chicken Soup

汽锅鸡

INGREDIENTS

½	chicken (500–600 g)
8	dried shiitake mushrooms, soaked to rehydrate
300 g	daikon
100 g	carrot
8	dried scallops, soaked to rehydrate
2 cm	Japanese leek, white part
2–3 slices	ginger, peeled
800 ml	chicken stock (page 139)
1 pinch	salt

During my training in China, I visited the Yunnan province where indirect heat is commonly used for cooking. I realised that such a method helps to retain the natural flavours of the ingredients. This dish makes use of a Yunnan steam pot, which allows steam from boiling water to pass through the funnel and into the covered pot to cook the soup.

METHOD

1. Debone the chicken and cut into chunks. Rinse well. Place the chicken in a pot of water and bring it to a boil. Remove from the heat and immerse in fresh water to rinse again. Drain and set aside.

2. Peel the daikon and carrot, then make decorative slits on the sides before cutting into 1–1.5-cm thick slices. Parboil lightly.

3. Put the chicken, mushrooms, daikon, carrot, dried scallops, Japanese leek, and ginger into a Yunnan steam pot. Add the chicken stock and season with salt. Cover with a lid.

4. Sit the Yunnan steam pot over the mouth of a larger pot filled with hot water and steam for 4 hours. Serve.

SERVES	8
PREPARATION TIME	30 minutes
COOKING TIME	2½ hours

Sautéed Pork, Scallop, and Daikon Soup

萝卜干贝猪肉汤

INGREDIENTS

120 g	pork
¼ tsp	salt
2 tsp	Shaoxing rice wine
1 dash	ground white pepper
3 Tbsp	potato starch
½	beaten egg
120 g	daikon
80 g	carrot
10 g	dried kelp, soaked to rehydrate
2 Tbsp	cooking oil
3 cm	Japanese leek, white part, chopped
2–3 slices	ginger, peeled
40 g	dried scallops, soaked to rehydrate

SOUP

800 ml	chicken stock (page 139)
1 Tbsp	Shaoxing rice wine
¼ tsp	salt
1 dash	ground white pepper

Although it is lesser known outside Szechwan, this soup is a popular favourite among the Szechwanese. When my father first introduced it in Japan, he incorporated dried kelp for an added umami taste. He also used potato starch and beaten egg to coat the pork and keep the meat tender.

METHOD

1. Cut the pork into 1-cm cubes and marinate with the salt, rice wine, pepper, potato starch, and beaten egg. Set aside.

2. Peel the daikon and carrot, then make decorative slits on the sides before cutting into 2-cm slices. Parboil until soft enough for a skewer to pass through easily.

3. Cut the dried kelp into fine strips.

4. Heat the oil in a pot until it reaches 160–170°C. Add the pork cubes one at a time and sauté, taking care that the cubes do not stick together.

5. Add the daikon, carrot, and dried kelp, followed by the ingredients for the soup.

6. Add the Japanese leek, ginger, and dried scallops, then seal the pot using cling wrap. Cover again with aluminium foil and place in a steamer. Steam for about 2½ hours. The soup is ready when it is clear and an umami flavour emerges. Serve.

SERVES 3–4
PREPARATION TIME 10 minutes
COOKING TIME 30 minutes

Steamed Chinese Cabbage with Scallop

干貝津白

INGREDIENTS

120 g	pork belly
200 g	Chinese cabbage
1 Tbsp	shallot oil
400 ml	chicken stock (page 139)
1 Tbsp	Shaoxing rice wine
1 pinch	sugar
1 tsp	chicken oil (page 139)
50 g	dried scallops, soaked to rehydrate
2–3 Tbsp	potato starch, mixed with a little water into a paste

SEASONING

1 tsp	sugar
1 pinch	salt
1 dash	ground white pepper
½ tsp	chicken seasoning powder

My father can't seem to get enough of this dish. A blend of sweet and savoury, it evokes a taste of home for us in the Chen family.

METHOD

1. Cut the pork into thin slices. Cut the cabbage into thin strips.

2. Heat the shallot oil in a pot over medium heat. Add the pork and sauté lightly, then add the cabbage and give it a quick stir.

3. Add the chicken stock, rice wine, sugar, chicken oil, and dried scallops. Cover the pot with aluminium foil and cook over low heat until the cabbage is translucent.

4. Add the seasoning and mix well.

5. Add the potato starch paste a little at a time and simmer to thicken the sauce. Serve.

Chengdu-style Vegetable Stew

成都素烩

SERVES	3–4
PREPARATION TIME	30 minutes
COOKING TIME	30 minutes

This is a traditional Szechwan dish made from freshly harvested vegetables that are in abundance in Chengdu. The combination of chicken and pork stock makes for a flavourful stew no matter what vegetables you add.

INGREDIENTS

30 g	daikon
20 g	carrot
40 g	pumpkin
40 g	potato
20 g	cucumber
150 g	Chinese cabbage
40 g	broccoli
20 g	gingko nuts
⅓ tsp	salt
1 dash	ground white pepper
3 Tbsp	potato starch, mixed with a little water into a paste
1 Tbsp	chicken oil (page 139)

STOCK

400 ml	chicken stock (page 139)
300 ml	pork stock (page 139)
1 Tbsp	Shaoxing rice wine
1 Tbsp	shallot oil
1 Tbsp	chicken oil (page 139)
½ tsp	sugar

METHOD

1. Peel the daikon and carrot, then make decorative slits on the sides before cutting into 5-mm thick slices. Peel the pumpkin and potato and cut into 5-mm thick slices. Cut the cucumber to the same size. Cut the cabbage into 1-cm x 6-cm pieces. Cut the broccoli into bite-sized pieces.

2. Parboil the daikon, carrot, pumpkin, potato, cabbage, broccoli, and gingko nuts. Add the cucumber last. Drain and set aside.

3. Combine all the ingredients for the stock in a pot and bring to a boil. Add the parboiled ingredients, except for the broccoli and cucumber, and simmer for 10 minutes over medium heat. Remove the pumpkin and potato from the pot once tender to prevent them from breaking apart.

4. Season with salt and pepper, then add the broccoli and cucumber to the pot. Stir in the potato starch paste and simmer to thicken the sauce.

5. Drizzle with chicken oil, then return the pumpkin and potato to the pot. Serve.

Sautéed Bok Choy and Duo Mushrooms with Black Truffle

黑松露炒双菇白菜

SERVES	3–4
PREPARATION TIME	10 minutes
COOKING TIME	10 minutes

INGREDIENTS

80 g	shiitake mushrooms
80 g	white button mushrooms
120 g	bok choy
3 g	black truffle, finely chopped
2 Tbsp	cooking oil
1 pinch	salt
1 dash	ground white pepper
1 tsp	truffle oil

SEASONING

15 g	sugar
10 g	Japanese soy sauce
10 g	oyster sauce
10 g	Chinese fermented rice (*jiuniang*)
30 ml	chicken stock (page 139)
1 dash	ground white pepper
10 g	potato starch, mixed with a little water into a paste

As a chef, I have tremendous respect for ingredients that elevate the flavour of any given produce with just the tiniest amount added. One such ingredient is the black truffle. Its earthy fragrance makes this vegetable dish truly unforgettable.

METHOD

1. Cut the mushrooms and bok choy into small bite-sized pieces.

2. Add the black truffle and seasoning. Mix well.

3. Heat the oil in a pan over medium heat. Add the mushrooms and sauté lightly. Remove from the pan.

4. Add the bok choy to the pan and sauté with salt and pepper. Transfer to a serving plate.

5. Return the mushrooms to the pan and add the seasoned black truffle.

6. Add the truffle oil and give it a quick stir. Arrange the mushrooms on the bok choy. Serve.

SERVES	3–4
PREPARATION TIME	10 minutes
COOKING TIME	20 minutes

Braised Tofu and Minced Pork with Chilli Bean Paste

家常豆腐

INGREDIENTS

350 g	firm tofu, drained
As needed	cooking oil
100 g	minced pork
1 tsp	chilli oil
1½ Tbsp	chilli bean paste (*doubanjiang*)
1 Tbsp	sweet bean paste (*tianmianjiang*)
10 cm	spring onion, sliced
2–3 slices	ginger, peeled
5 g	Japanese spring onion, finely chopped
2 Tbsp	potato starch, mixed with a little water into a paste

SEASONING

300–350 ml	chicken stock (page 139)
1 Tbsp	Shaoxing rice wine
½ Tbsp	Japanese soy sauce
1 tsp	sugar
1 dash	ground white pepper

At our Shisen Hanten restaurants in Japan, the braised tofu and minced pork with chilli bean paste comes second only to Chen's *mapo* tofu. Full-flavoured and protein-packed, this delicacy goes wonderfully with a steaming bowl of rice.

METHOD

1. Slice the tofu into 1-cm thick rectangular slices.

2. Heat sufficient oil for deep-frying in a wok to 180–200°C. Gently lower the tofu into the hot oil and deep-fry until golden and crisp on the outside.

3. Drain the oil from the pot and reheat with 2 Tbsp fresh oil. Add the minced pork and sauté lightly.

4. Add the chilli oil, chilli bean paste, and sweet bean paste, and mix well.

5. Add the spring onion and ginger, and mix again.

6. Add the seasoning and tofu. Simmer over low heat for 5–6 minutes to allow the flavours to blend.

7. Add the Japanese spring onion, followed by the potato starch paste to thicken the sauce. Transfer to a serving dish.

8. Heat 1 Tbsp oil and drizzle it over the tofu. Serve.

SERVES	3–4
PREPARATION TIME	10 minutes
COOKING TIME	20 minutes

Chen Kenmin's Mapo Tofu

陈建民式麻婆豆腐

INGREDIENTS

350 g	silken tofu
1 pinch	salt
As needed	cooking oil
100 g	minced pork
150 ml	chicken stock (page 139)
1 Tbsp	Shaoxing rice wine
1 Tbsp	Japanese soy sauce
1 dash	ground white pepper
20 g	Japanese leek, white part, chopped
2 Tbsp	potato starch, mixed with a little water into a paste

SAUCE

1 Tbsp	chilli bean paste (*doubanjiang*)
1 Tbsp	sweet bean paste (*tianmianjiang*)
1 tsp	fermented black beans (*douchi*), minced
1 tsp	grated garlic

When my grandfather first introduced *mapo* tofu in Japan, he omitted the Szechwan peppers and added more sweet bean paste to suit the milder palate of his audiences back then. His version of this iconic dish was monumental in laying the foundation for the success of the Shisen Hanten brand. I am honoured to have this opportunity to share his recipe with you.

METHOD

1. Cut the tofu into 2-cm cubes and boil in a pot of lightly salted water for about 1 minute. Drain well.

2. Heat some oil in a pan over medium heat. Add the minced pork and sauté until the juices have evaporated and clear fat emerges.

3. Add the ingredients for the sauce in the order listed and sauté until fragrant.

4. Add the chicken stock and tofu. Bring to a boil, stirring slowly.

5. Add the rice wine, soy sauce, and pepper, and simmer until the sauce is flavourful.

6. Add the Japanese leek, then stir in the potato starch paste to thicken the sauce. Transfer to a serving dish.

7. Heat 1 Tbsp oil and drizzle it over the dish. Serve.

Boil the tofu in lightly salted water for about 1 minute.

Add the ingredients for the sauce to the minced pork and sauté until fragrant.

Add the potato starch paste to thicken the sauce.

Chen Family's Mapo Tofu

陈麻婆豆腐

SERVES 3–4
PREPARATION TIME 10 minutes
COOKING TIME 20 minutes

INGREDIENTS

350 g	firm tofu
1 pinch	salt
As needed	cooking oil
80 g	minced pork
150 ml	chicken stock (page 139)
15 g	Japanese spring onion
1 Tbsp	Shaoxing rice wine
1 tsp	Japanese soy sauce
1 dash	ground white pepper
20 g	Japanese leek, white part, chopped
2 Tbsp	potato starch, mixed with a little water into a paste
1 tsp	Szechwan pepper oil
½ tsp	red Szechwan peppercorns

SAUCE

1 Tbsp	chilli bean paste (*doubanjiang*)
½ Tbsp	sweet bean paste (*tianmianjiang*)
2 tsp	fermented black beans (*douchi*), minced
1 tsp	grated garlic
1 Tbsp	chilli powder
1 Tbsp	chilli oil

Unlike its predecessor, this updated rendition of my family's *mapo* tofu recipe presents bolder flavours. The use of red Szechwan peppercorns gives it that distinct numbing flavour unique to Szechwan cuisine. To this day, we only use chilli bean paste that is specially fermented and aged in the Szechwan province for at least three years.

METHOD

1. Cut the tofu into 2-cm cubes and boil in a pot of lightly salted water for about 1 minute. Drain well.

2. Heat some oil in a pan over medium heat. Add the minced pork and sauté until the juice from the pork has evaporated and clear fat emerges.

3. Add the ingredients for the sauce in the order listed and sauté until fragrant.

4. Add the stock, tofu, and Japanese spring onion. Bring to a boil, stirring slowly.

5. Add the rice wine, soy sauce, and pepper, and simmer until the sauce is flavourful.

6. Add the Japanese leek, then stir in the potato starch paste to thicken the sauce.

7. Stir in the Szechwan pepper oil. Sprinkle with peppercorns. Transfer to a serving dish and serve.

Meat & Poultry

SERVES 3–4
PREPARATION TIME 10 minutes
COOKING TIME 40 minutes

Pork with Spicy Garlic Sauce

云白肉

INGREDIENTS

500 g	pork (hind leg)
2	cucumbers
1–2 Tbsp	Szechwan pepper oil

SAUCE

50 ml	sweet soy sauce (*tianjiangyou*)
2 Tbsp	Japanese soy sauce
15 g	grated garlic
1 tsp	Japanese rice vinegar

I n Chinese, the name of this dish means "white cloud meat" in reference to the tender texture of the boiled pork strips. When preparing this dish, try to slice the cucumbers and boiled pork as thinly as possible, making light and translucent strips.

METHOD

1. Boil the pork in a large pot of water for 20–30 minutes. Leave the pork to cool in the pot.

2. Slice the cucumbers thinly and soak in iced water until crisp. Drain.

3. Make scores on the fat of the cooled pork, then cut the pork into thin slices. Arrange on a serving plate. Top with the sliced cucumbers.

4. Combine the ingredients for the sauce and pour it over the cucumbers and pork.

5. Drizzle the Szechwan pepper oil over the dish and serve.

Marinate the beef.

Slice the capsicum and bamboo shoot into thin strips.

Combine the ingredients for the seasoning.

SERVES	3–4
PREPARATION TIME	20 minutes
COOKING TIME	10 minutes

Stir-fried Beef with Green Capsicum and Bamboo Shoot

青椒笋丝炒牛肉

INGREDIENTS

80 g	beef (round steak)
80 g	green capsicum
20 g	boiled bamboo shoot
As needed	cooking oil
15 g	Japanese leek, white part, chopped

MARINADE

1 pinch	salt
1 dash	ground white pepper
1 Tbsp	Shaoxing rice wine
1 tsp	Japanese soy sauce
1	beaten egg
1 Tbsp	potato starch
1 Tbsp	cooking oil

SEASONING

½ tsp	sugar
1 Tbsp	Shaoxing rice wine
1 Tbsp	Japanese soy sauce
½ tsp	oyster sauce
1 dash	ground white pepper
1 Tbsp	chicken stock (page 139)
1 Tbsp	potato starch, mixed with a little water into a paste

Being able to successfully recreate this dish is a rite of passage for any Shisen Hanten chef in training. My dad could not emphasise enough the importance of mastering this particular dish because it covers a variety of preparation and cooking techniques. I can now fully appreciate where he was coming from. When executed properly, this dish brings a great sense of accomplishment to the chef.

METHOD

1. Slice the beef into thin strips. Add the marinade and mix well.

2. Slice the capsicum and bamboo shoot into thin strips.

3. Combine the ingredients for the seasoning and set aside.

4. Heat some oil in a wok to 120°C. Add the marinated beef and sauté, using the spatula to separate the strips.

5. Add the capsicum and bamboo shoot, and give it a quick stir.

6. Drain any excess oil from the wok. Add the Japanese leek, followed by the seasoning. Sauté briskly. Transfer to a serving dish.

7. Heat 1 Tbsp oil and drizzle it over the dish. Serve.

SERVES 3–4
PREPARATION TIME 1 hour
COOKING TIME 20 minutes

Twice-cooked Pork

回
锅
肉

INGREDIENTS

150 g	pork belly
140 g	green cabbage
100 g	green capsicum
50 g	Japanese leek, white part
50 g	Japanese spring onion
As needed	cooking oil
1 Tbsp	chilli oil

SEASONING A

1 tsp	fermented black beans (*douchi*), minced
½ tsp	grated garlic
½ Tbsp	Chinese fermented rice (*jiuniang*)
⅔ Tbsp	chilli bean paste (*doubanjiang*)

SEASONING B

⅔ Tbsp	sweet bean paste (*tianmianjiang*)
1 Tbsp	Shaoxing rice wine
½ Tbsp	Japanese soy sauce
1 dash	ground white pepper

My grandfather liked to prepare this at home when I was young. Back then, garlic scapes were not widely available in Japan, so cabbage was used as a substitute. I am proud to say that my grandfather's version of twice-cooked pork has become one of the best loved dishes in Japan.

METHOD

1. Boil the pork in a large pot of water until the juices run clear when the pork is pricked with a skewer. Cut the pork into 2-mm thick slices.

2. Cut and discard the core from the cabbage, then cut the leaves into bite-sized pieces. Cut the capsicum into strips. Cut the Japanese leek diagonally into 5-mm slices. Cut the Japanese spring onion into 3-cm lengths.

3. Heat some oil in a wok over medium heat. Add the cabbage and sauté lightly. Transfer the cabbage to a plate. Drain any excess oil from the wok.

4. Place the pork in the wok slice by slice and avoid overlapping them. Allow to brown on both sides.

5. Add the capsicum and Japanese leek, and sauté.

6. Add seasoning A and sauté until fragrant. Return the cabbage to the wok. Add the Japanese spring onion.

7. Add seasoning B and simmer over low heat for the flavours to blend.

8. Add the chilli oil and give it a quick stir. Transfer to a serving plate and serve.

SERVES 6–8
PREPARATION TIME 8–10 hours
COOKING TIME 1½ hours

Szechwan-style Tea-smoked Duck

樟茶鴨

In the early days of Shisen Hanten, the lack of kitchen space and equipment forced my grandfather to improvise and smoke the duck meat out in his garden. Before it was served in the restaurant, my grandmother, Chen Yoko, would always sample it first to ensure it was up to standard. It also happens to be her favourite dish.

INGREDIENTS

1	duck
As needed	cooking oil

NITRATE SALT WATER

3.4 litres	water
30 g	black tea leaves
300 g	salt
30 g	nitrate (curing salt)
30 g	star anise
30 g	cinnamon
5 g	red Szechwan peppercorns
30 g	Japanese leek, green part
10 g	ginger

FOR SMOKING

200 g	*hinoki* leaves
200 g	uncooked rice
20 g	black tea leaves
100 g	sugar

METHOD

1. Start preparations a day ahead.

2. Prepare the nitrate salt water. In a pot, simmer 400 ml water with the tea leaves to make a thick tea. In another pot, boil 3 litres with the other ingredients until the salt is dissolved. Leave to cool, then combine the two solutions.

3. Soak the duck in the nitrate salt water for 8–10 hours. The soaking time can be shorter in the summer and longer in the winter.

4. Remove the duck and place in a pot of boiling water for 1–2 minutes. Drain the duck and pat dry.

5. Line the base of a large pot with aluminium foil. Place the ingredients for smoking on the foil and top with a grilling rack. Place the duck on the rack. Cover the pot with a lid and fill any gaps with a towel. Place the pot over medium heat for 10 minutes, then turn off the heat and let the duck sit for another 10 minutes.

6. Remove the duck and place in a steamer to steam for 1 hour. Pat dry the duck and set aside to cool.

7. Heat sufficient oil for deep-frying to 170°C. Lower the duck into the oil and cook over medium heat until the duck begins to float. Increase to high heat and fry until the skin is crispy.

8. Debone the duck and slice. Arrange on a serving plate and serve.

1. Score the pork with criss-cross cuts.

2. Squeeze the pork into balls.

3. Dice the onion very finely.

SERVES	3–4
PREPARATION TIME	20 minutes
COOKING TIME	10 minutes

Sweet and Sour Pork with Black Vinegar

黑醋咕咾肉

INGREDIENTS

300 g	pork shoulder
1 pinch	salt
1 dash	ground white pepper
1 dash	Japanese soy sauce
1 Tbsp	Shaoxing rice wine
2 Tbsp	beaten egg
2½ Tbsp	potato starch
80 g	onion
50 g	red capsicum
50 g	yellow capsicum
50 g	green capsicum
As needed	cooking oil

SAUCE

100 ml	balsamic vinegar
6 Tbsp	sugar
100 ml	water
1½ Tbsp	honey
1⅔ Tbsp	vincotto
2½ Tbsp	Japanese soy sauce
3 Tbsp	Zhenjiang vinegar
2 Tbsp	Japanese rice vinegar
2 Tbsp	potato starch, mixed with a little water into a paste

Here I mix Chinese black vinegar, Japanese rice vinegar, Italian balsamic vinegar, and vincotto (cooked Italian wine) for a new take on an old favourite. When done right, the sauce coating the crisp outer layer will seep into the moist tender pork underneath. Remember to score the pork to achieve a softer texture.

METHOD

1. Score the pork with criss-cross cuts, then cut it into 12 bite-sized cubes (25 g per cube).

2. Marinate the meat with the salt, pepper, soy sauce, and rice wine, then add the beaten egg, followed by the potato starch. Use your hand to squeeze each piece of pork into a ball. Set aside.

3. Dice the onion and capsicums very finely. Place in a bowl of cold water and leave to soak for 20–30 minutes. Drain and arrange on a serving plate.

4. Prepare the sauce. Boil the balsamic vinegar until it is reduced by half. Add the remaining ingredients except for the two vinegars and potato starch. Bring to a boil. Let the mixture cool, then add both the vinegars.

5. Heat sufficient oil for deep-frying to 160°C and deep-fry the pork for 3–4 minutes. Increase the heat to 190°C and continue frying the pork until it is crispy. Remove and drain.

6. Heat the sauce, then stir in the potato starch paste to thicken the sauce. Add the fried pork and mix in some oil.

7. Arrange the fried pork on a serving plate with the diced onion and capsicums. Serve.

黑
醋
咕
咾
肉

Stir-fried Yuxiang Pork

魚香肉丝

SERVES	3–4
PREPARATION TIME	20 minutes
COOKING TIME	10 minutes

INGREDIENTS

30 g	dried *gong choy*
110 g	pork loin
30 g	dried shiitake mushrooms, soaked to rehydrate
40 g	boiled bamboo shoot
10 cm	Japanese leek, white part
As needed	cooking oil
1 Tbsp	chilli bean paste (*doubanjiang*)

MARINADE

2 tsp	Shaoxing rice wine
½ tsp	Japanese soy sauce
1 pinch	salt
1 dash	ground white pepper
1½ Tbsp	beaten egg
1 Tbsp	potato starch, mixed with a little water into a paste
2 tsp	cooking oil

SEASONING

1 Tbsp	sugar
1 Tbsp	chicken stock (page 139)
1 Tbsp	Shaoxing rice wine
1 Tbsp	Japanese rice vinegar
1 Tbsp	Chinese fermented rice (*jiuniang*)
⅔ Tbsp	Japanese soy sauce
1 dash	ground white pepper
2 tsp	grated ginger
1⅓ tsp	grated garlic
1 Tbsp	potato starch, mixed with a little water into a paste

Gong choy is a type of wild vegetable popular in China since the Qing Dynasty. If unavailable in your local supermarket, this crisp vegetable can be substituted with like-textured vegetables such as stem lettuce and asparagus.

METHOD

1. Start preparations for this dish a day ahead. Soak the dried *gong choy* in water overnight. Drain and cut into 6-cm lengths.

2. Slice the pork into 3-mm thick strips and marinate with the rice wine, soy sauce, salt, and pepper. Add the beaten egg and mix well by hand. Add the potato starch paste and oil, and mix well. Set aside.

3. Cut the mushrooms into 3-mm thick slices. Cut the bamboo shoot into 6-cm x 3-mm strips. Finely dice the Japanese leek.

4. Heat some oil in a wok to 130–140°C. Add the pork and spread the strips out using chopsticks. Add the mushrooms, bamboo shoot, and dried *gong choy* one item at a time, stirring briskly after each addition. Transfer to a plate and set aside.

5. Drain the oil from the wok. Add 1 Tbsp fresh oil, Japanese leek, and chilli bean paste. Sauté until fragrant.

6. Return the mushrooms, bamboo shoot, and dried *gong choy* to the wok. Add the seasoning and sauté. Drizzle with 1 Tbsp oil. Transfer to a serving plate and serve.

Steamed Pork Belly with Preserved Szechwan Mustard Greens

芽菜扣肉

SERVES	6
PREPARATION TIME	20 minutes
COOKING TIME	3 hours

While it takes some effort to prepare, this Szechwan classic is sure to be a hit at any gathering. When steaming, I prefer to use a bamboo steamer for its ability to absorb moisture and prevent ingredients from getting soggy. I also find that it adds more interesting flavours to the dish.

INGREDIENTS

800 g	pork belly
2–3	Japanese leeks, white part
4–5 slices	ginger, peeled
As needed	water
2–3 Tbsp	light soy sauce
1 litre	cooking oil
150 g	soy bean sprouts
100 g	Szechwan preserved mustard greens (*ya cai*)
1 Tbsp	shallot oil
1 Tbsp	sugar
1 Tbsp	Shaoxing rice wine

SEASONING

1 Tbsp	sweet soy sauce (*tianjiangyou*)
2½ Tbsp	sugar
2 Tbsp	light soy sauce
12 Tbsp	water
1 tsp	Chinese fermented rice (*jiuniang*)

METHOD

1. Place the pork belly, Japanese leeks, and ginger in a pot. Add a generous amount of water and boil until the pork is evenly heated. Remove the pork and discard the other ingredients. Spread the soy sauce on the pork skin.

2. Heat the oil in a wok until very hot, then place the boiled pork skin-side down in the wok. Cook for about 1 minute. Remove from the heat.

3. Cut the soy bean sprouts and preserved mustard greens into 3-cm lengths. Heat the shallot oil in a wok over medium heat. Add the vegetables, sugar, and rice wine, and sauté until fragrant, then spread them out in a bamboo steamer and steam for 30 minutes.

4. Cut the pork belly into 7-mm thick slices and use the slices to line a small bowl. Place the steamed vegetables in the lined bowl and pack firmly.

5. Mix the ingredients for the seasoning, then pour it into the bowl. Wrap the bowl with cling wrap and steam for 1 hour 40 minutes to 2 hours, until the pork is very tender.

6. Unmould the contents of the bowl onto a serving plate. Garnish as desired and serve.

SERVES	10
PREPARATION TIME	36 hours
COOKING TIME	40 minutes

Steamed Beef with Toasted Rice Powder

粉蒸牛肉

INGREDIENTS

500 g	beef (round steak)
15 g	grated ginger
10 g	red Szechwan pepper
75 g	toasted rice powder
1 Tbsp	cooking oil
1	lotus leaf

TOASTED RICE POWDER

140 g	uncooked rice
60 g	uncooked glutinous rice
2 Tbsp	five-spice powder

MARINADE

10 g	chilli bean paste (*doubanjiang*)
100 g	Chinese fermented rice (*jiuniang*)
10 g	chilli powder
50 ml	Japanese soy sauce
1 pinch	salt
1 Tbsp	sweet soy sauce (*tianjiangyou*)
½ tsp	white fermented bean curd
½ Tbsp	Shaoxing rice wine

SEASONING

10 g	grated garlic
15 g	toasted rice powder
1 dash	*lao you*

GARNISHING

20 g	minced onion
2–3 sprigs	coriander leaves
1	spring onion, finely chopped

This showcases a preparation method unique to Szechwan cuisine, where rice powder is used to coat meat before cooking. By doing so, the taste of the meat is absorbed into the rice powder, adding texture and flavour that are immediately apparent from the first bite.

METHOD

1. Prepare the toasted rice powder up to 2 days ahead. Wash the rice thoroughly and immerse in a basin of water for about 12 hours. Drain the rice and spread it out on a tray to dry for 12–24 hours. Place the dried rice in a food processor. Add the five-spice powder and grind until fine.

2. Cut the beef into thin strips and rub in the marinade, grated ginger, and red Szechwan pepper. Add the toasted rice powder, followed by the oil. Mix well.

3. Line a bamboo steamer with the lotus leaf. Trim to fit. Add the beef to the lined steamer and steam for 30–40 minutes.

4. Combine the ingredients for the seasoning and pour it over the steamed beef. Garnish with the minced onion, coriander leaves, and spring onion. Serve.

Add the potato starch paste and mix gently, being careful not to break the meat.

Add the chilli oil and mix gently again.

Heat the oil and drizzle it over the dish.

SERVES	3–4
PREPARATION TIME	15 minutes
COOKING TIME	15 minutes

Poached Sliced Beef in Hot Chilli Oil

水煮牛肉

Remember to add the hot chilli oil as the last step to finish this dish. It will intensify the spiciness of the chilli and fuse the flavours of the ingredients more cohesively.

INGREDIENTS

130 g	beef fillet
1 pinch	salt
1 dash	ground white pepper
½ Tbsp	Shaoxing rice wine
1 tsp	Japanese soy sauce
3 Tbsp	potato starch, mixed with a little water into a paste
1 Tbsp	chilli oil
60 g	*xiao bai cai*
60 g	celery
80 g	Chinese cabbage
As needed	cooking oil
5 g	facing heaven peppers
2 g	red Szechwan peppercorns
40 g	soy bean sprouts
2 Tbsp	chilli bean paste (*doubanjiang*)
350 ml	chicken stock (page 139)
2–3 sprigs	coriander leaves

SEASONING

½ tsp	sugar
1 dash	ground white pepper
1 Tbsp	Shaoxing rice wine
2 tsp	Japanese soy sauce
2 tsp	chilli oil

METHOD

1. Slice the beef into thin, bite-sized pieces. Season with the salt, pepper, rice wine, and soy sauce. Mix gently, taking care not to break the meat. Add the potato starch paste and mix gently, followed by the chilli oil.

2. Slice the *xiao bai cai*, celery, and cabbage into bite-sized pieces.

3. Heat 2 Tbsp cooking oil into a pot. Add the facing heaven peppers and peppercorns, and sauté over low heat until fragrant. Remove and cut the facing heaven peppers into fine strips. Leave the oil in the pot.

4. Add the *xiao bai cai*, celery, cabbage, soy bean sprouts, and chilli bean paste to the pot. Sauté over low heat until fragrant.

5. Add the chicken stock and the seasoning, except for the chilli oil. Bring to a boil, then lower the heat to simmer.

6. Add the seasoned beef, one piece at a time, spreading the meat out and stirring slowly until the meat is done.

7. Add the chilli oil, sliced facing heaven peppers, and peppercorns.

8. Heat about 4 Tbsp oil and drizzle it over the dish. Garnish with coriander leaves and serve.

SERVES	3–4
PREPARATION TIME	10 minutes
COOKING TIME	10 minutes

Daqian Chicken

大千鸡块

INGREDIENTS

50 g	celery
30 g	shiitake mushrooms
20 g	green capsicum
20 g	red capsicum
1	Japanese leek, white part
2-cm knob	ginger
200 g	chicken thigh
⅓ Tbsp	salt
1 dash	ground white pepper
1 tsp	Shaoxing rice wine
½	beaten egg
2 Tbsp	potato starch
As needed	cooking oil
8 g	facing heaven peppers
8–10	red Szechwan peppercorns
½ Tbsp	chilli bean paste (*doubanjiang*)
30 ml	chilli oil

SEASONING

1 Tbsp	sugar
1 Tbsp	Chinese fermented rice (*jiuniang*)
1 Tbsp	Shaoxing rice wine
1 Tbsp	Japanese soy sauce
2 tsp	Japanese rice vinegar
2 Tbsp	chicken stock (page 139)
1 dash	ground white pepper
1 Tbsp	grated ginger
⅔ Tbsp	potato starch, mixed with a little water into a paste

This dish is said to be a favourite of the renowned Szechwan painter, Zhang Daqian. It showcases the full range of Szechwan flavours, from tartness and sweetness, to tongue-numbing spiciness.

METHOD

1. Cut the celery into 2-cm lengths. Make decorative cuts on the mushroom caps. Cut the capsicums into 1.5-cm squares. Cut the Japanese leek into 1.5-cm lengths. Peel the ginger and slice thinly.

2. Cut the chicken into large bite-sized pieces and season with the salt, pepper, rice wine, and beaten egg. Coat with potato starch.

3. Heat sufficient oil for deep-frying in a wok to 160–170°C. Add the chicken and deep-fry until crispy.

4. Add the celery, mushrooms, and capsicums to the wok. Drain the oil and set the cooked vegetables aside.

5. Add fresh oil to the wok and sauté the facing heaven peppers and peppercorns.

6. Add the chilli bean paste and sauté over low heat.

7. Add the Japanese leek and ginger.

8. Arrange on a serving plate. Drizzle with chilli oil and serve.

SERVES	3–4
PREPARATION TIME	30 minutes
COOKING TIME	10 minutes

Sautéed Beef with Cumin

孜
然
牛
柳

INGREDIENTS

160 g	beef fillet
50 g	barbecue sauce
As needed	cornstarch
As needed	cooking oil
15 g	*lao you*
20 g	grated garlic
20 g	facing heaven peppers
1 g	green Szechwan peppercorns
1 tsp	cumin
1 tsp	chicken seasoning powder
1 pinch	sugar

Shisen Hanten's interpretation of the classic Hunan favourite uses beef fillet, breaded and fried, with green Szechwan peppercorns and facing heaven peppers for an added kick.

METHOD

1. Cut the beef fillet into 8 pieces, each about 20 g.

2. Rub the beef with barbecue sauce and set aside to marinate for 20 minutes.

3. Drain excess moisture from the beef, then coat with a thick layer of cornstarch.

4. Heat sufficient oil for deep-frying in a wok to 170°C. Sprinkle the beef with a little water, then deep-fry until crispy. Remove and set aside.

5. Drain the oil from the wok and add fresh oil. Add the *lao you*, garlic, facing heaven peppers, and peppercorns. Sauté over low heat until fragrant.

6. Return the beef to the wok. Add the cumin, chicken seasoning powder, and sugar, and mix carefully to avoid breaking the coating of the beef. Arrange on a serving plate and serve.

Slice the chicken thighs to even out the thickness.

Season the chicken with salt, pepper, soy sauce, and rice wine.

Coat the chicken with cornstarch.

SERVES 3–4
PREPARATION TIME 10 minutes
COOKING TIME 10 minutes

Crispy Chilli Chicken 辣子鸡

INGREDIENTS

200 g	chicken thighs, deboned
3 g	salt
1 dash	ground white pepper
⅓ tsp	Japanese soy sauce
50 ml	Shaoxing rice wine
As needed	cornstarch
1 Tbsp	*lao you*
25 g	facing heaven peppers
1 g	red Szechwan peppercorns
1 g	green Szechwan peppercorns
20 g	Japanese spring onion, thinly sliced
5 g	ginger, peeled and cut into 1-cm squares
3 g	sugar
3 g	chicken seasoning powder

This is a simpler version of *la zi ji* (crispy chilli chicken), one of Shisen Hanten's most popular signature dishes. I use a boneless cut of chicken, and season and coat it with cornstarch before deep-frying. The traditional preparation method uses chicken with bones, and the chicken is deep-fried without any coating.

METHOD

1. Slice the chicken thighs to even out the thickness, then cut each thigh in half.

2. Score the thighs with criss-cross cuts, then cut into 3-cm pieces.

3. Place the chicken in a bowl and season with salt, pepper, soy sauce, and rice wine. Coat with cornstarch.

4. Heat sufficient oil for deep-frying in a wok to 160°C. Deep-fry the chicken until crispy. Remove and set aside.

5. Drain the oil from the wok. Add the *lao you*, facing heaven peppers, and peppercorns. Sauté over low heat until fragrant.

6. Add the Japanese spring onion and ginger. Sauté lightly, then return the chicken to the wok.

7. Add the sugar and chicken seasoning powder, and give it a quick stir. Arrange on a serving plate and serve.

SERVES	3–4
PREPARATION TIME	10 minutes
COOKING TIME	15 minutes

Szechwan-style Stewed Chicken in a Hot Stone Bowl

石锅土鸡

INGREDIENTS

200 g	chicken thighs
20 g	shiitake mushrooms
40 g	*maitake* mushrooms
40 g	white enoki mushrooms
As needed	cooking oil
2 cloves	garlic, peeled and sliced
1-cm knob	ginger, peeled and sliced
4	hawk claw chillies (*takanotsume* peppers), sliced in half, seeds removed
600 ml	chicken stock (page 139)
20 g	dried glass noodles, soaked to rehydrate
1 Tbsp	chilli oil
1 Tbsp	Shaoxing rice wine
10 g	spring onions, chopped

SEASONING

1 dash	chicken seasoning powder
1 dash	ground white pepper
1 pinch	sugar
1 dash	five-spice powder
1 Tbsp	chicken oil (page 139)
1½ Tbsp	oyster sauce

This dish uses hawk claw chilli which was named for its talon shape. Known in Japan as *takanotsume*, this variety is particularly hot. The sweet and aromatic five-spice powder, said to balance flavours according to the Chinese philosophies of yin and yang, also adds a special twist to the dish. I serve the dish in a hot stone bowl, which helps keep it hot and spicy for a longer time.

METHOD

1. Slice the chicken thighs into equal halves. Cut each half into strips, then slice each strip into rectangular pieces.

2. Mince the shiitake mushrooms. Use your hands to tear apart the *maitake* and enoki mushrooms.

3. Heat 500 ml oil in a pan over high heat. Add the shiitake and *maitake* mushrooms, then remove them with a strainer. Discard the oil.

4. Reheat the pan with 1 Tbsp oil and sauté the chicken until it is just cooked on the outside. Add the garlic, ginger, and hawk claw chillies, and sauté until aromatic.

5. Add the chicken stock and seasoning. Simmer over low heat for 5–7 minutes.

6. Add the enoki mushrooms and glass noodles, then simmer for 2–3 minutes for the flavours to develop. Add the chilli oil.

7. Heat a stone bowl, then add the rice wine and heat until aromatic. Transfer the chicken and mushroom mixture to the bowl. Top with the chopped spring onions and serve.

Seafood 海鮮

Sauté the ingredients until fragrant.

Braise the lobster for 2–3 minutes.

Stir the beaten egg into the sauce.

Stir-fried Lobster with Chilli Sauce

干烧龙虾

SERVES	3–4
PREPARATION TIME	10 minutes
COOKING TIME	15 minutes

INGREDIENTS

1	lobster
1 pinch	salt
1 dash	ground white pepper
As needed	Shaoxing rice wine
As needed	potato starch
As needed	cooking oil
2 Tbsp	chilli bean paste (*doubanjiang*)
4 Tbsp	ketchup
1 Tbsp	Chinese fermented rice (*jiuniang*)
1 Tbsp	grated ginger
1 tsp	grated garlic
400 ml	chicken stock (page 139)
1/2 Tbsp	sugar
50 g	Japanese leek, white part, finely chopped
1 Tbsp	potato starch, mixed with a little water into a paste
1	beaten egg
2 tsp	Japanese rice vinegar

I use ketchup to balance out the spiciness of this dish, and eggs to soften its texture. Make sure you get the timing just right when cooking the lobster, so the meat does not turn tough or chewy.

METHOD

1. Cut the lobster lengthwise in half. Season with salt, pepper, and 1 tsp rice wine. Coat with potato starch.

2. Heat sufficient oil for deep-frying in a wok to 170°C. Add the lobster and turn off the heat. Let it sit for 7–8 minutes. Remove the lobster and discard the oil.

3. Add 2 Tbsp fresh oil to the wok. Add the chilli bean paste, ketchup, Chinese fermented rice, grated ginger, and grated garlic. Sauté until fragrant.

4. Add the lobster, chicken stock, 1 Tbsp rice wine, and sugar. Braise for 2–3 minutes.

5. Add the Japanese leek, then stir in the potato starch paste to thicken the sauce.

6. Add the beaten egg and stir it into the sauce. Increase to high heat. Add the rice vinegar.

7. Arrange the lobster on a serving plate and serve.

干烧龙虾

SERVES	6
PREPARATION TIME	40 minutes
COOKING TIME	20 minutes

Turbot with Shishito Pepper

日本青椒多宝鱼

I prepare this using fried fish, a style that is currently very popular with Szechwan restaurants. You will find the broth is rich and tasty, yet light enough to enjoy as soup.

INGREDIENTS

1 kg	turbot, scaled and gutted
100 g	lotus root, sliced
100 g	potatoes, peeled and sliced
2 Tbsp	shallot oil
100 g	shallots, peeled and halved
40 g	onion, peeled and sliced
100 g	soy bean sprouts
300 ml	chicken stock (page 139)
300 ml	pork stock (page 139)
1 Tbsp	Shaoxing rice wine
1 Tbsp	sugar
1 tsp	chicken seasoning powder
1 dash	ground white pepper
2 Tbsp	Szechwan pepper oil
300 g	shishito peppers, sliced

MARINADE

2 Tbsp	Shaoxing rice wine
½ Tbsp	salt
10 g	green Szechwan peppercorns
2–3 stalks	Japanese leek, white part
3–4 slices	ginger, peeled

SEASONING

10 g	grated garlic
20 g	grated ginger
½ Tbsp	chilli powder
1 Tbsp	Szechwan preserved mustard greens (ya cai)
2 Tbsp	white fermented bean curd
2 Tbsp	chilli oil

METHOD

1. Place the turbot in a deep dish. Combine the ingredients for the marinade and pour it over the turbot. Rub the Japanese leek and ginger into the fish. Set aside for 30 minutes.

2. Heat sufficient oil for deep-frying in a wok to 180°C. Remove the fish from the marinade and lower it into the hot oil. Deep-fry until crispy. Remove and set aside.

3. Add the lotus root and potatoes to the wok, and fry lightly. Remove and set aside.

4. Heat the shallot oil in another wok and lightly sauté the shallots, onion, and soy bean sprouts. Add the seasoning and sauté until fragrant.

5. Add the chicken and pork stocks, and bring it to a boil.

6. Add the fish, rice wine, sugar, chicken seasoning powder, and pepper. Cook over low heat for 2–3 minutes.

7. Arrange the cooked vegetables on a serving plate and place the fish on top. Pour the sauce over the fish.

8. Heat the Szechwan pepper oil in another wok and lightly sauté the shishito peppers until fragrant. Arrange on the fish and serve.

Coral Trout Topped with Home-made Chilli Paste

剁椒东星斑

SERVES	4
PREPARATION TIME	10 minutes + 2 weeks' refrigeration
COOKING TIME	20 minutes

I personally favour steaming trout in soy sauce as it brings out the natural sweetness of the fish. My home-made chilli paste is icing on the proverbial cake for those looking for a more spicy kick without the numbing spiciness typical of Szechwan peppercorns.

INGREDIENTS

1	coral trout (600–800 g), scaled and gutted
1 dash	salt
1 dash	ground white pepper
1–2 Tbsp	shallot oil
1	onion, peeled and chopped
2–3 slices	ginger, peeled
2–3	dried shiso leaves
250 ml	seasoned soy sauce for seafood
2–3	spring onions, finely chopped
30–50 ml	peanut oil

HOME-MADE CHILLI PASTE

250 g	red chillies, finely chopped
120 g	grated garlic
15 g	grated ginger
15 g	sugar
7 g	salt
20 ml	sake

METHOD

1. Prepare the home-made chilli paste 2 weeks ahead. Place the ingredients in a large bowl and mix well. Transfer to an airtight glass jar and leave to ferment in the refrigerator for 2 weeks.

2. Pat dry the fish thoroughly, including the gills.

3. Season the fish with the salt and pepper, then coat it with shallot oil. Place on a steaming plate.

4. Place the onion, ginger, and dried shiso leaves on the fish, then steam for 15–20 minutes.

5. Remove the onion, ginger, and dried shiso leaves from the fish, and arrange the fish on a serving plate.

6. Bring the seasoned soy sauce for seafood to a boil and pour it over the fish. Top the fish with the home-made chilli paste and chopped spring onions.

7. Heat the peanut oil to 200°C and pour it over the fish. Serve.

SERVES 3–4
PREPARATION TIME 10 minutes
COOKING TIME 10 minutes

Stir-fried Squid with Cream Sauce

奶油醬鱿花

INGREDIENTS

200 g	squid tubes
35 g	green courgettes
As needed	cooking oil
10 g	Japanese leek, white part, cut into 1-cm lengths
2 g	ginger, peeled and thinly sliced
1 Tbsp	palm oil

SAUCE

½ tsp	sugar
¼ tsp	salt
1 dash	ground white pepper
100 ml	evaporated milk
1½ tsp	Shaoxing rice wine
80 ml	chicken stock (page 139)
1–1½ tsp	potato starch, mixed with a little water into a paste

Palm oil is rich in carotene, and it is what gives this dish its lovely orange hue. You want to be mindful of cooking the squid just right to attain the perfect texture.

METHOD

1. Cut the squid tubes open and flatten using the flat side of a chopper. Score with criss-cross cuts, then slice each tube lengthwise in half. Cut into bite-sized pieces.

2. Cut the courgettes into pieces the same size as the squid.

3. Combine the ingredients for the sauce.

4. Heat some oil in a wok to 140–150°C. Add the squid and cook until about 70 per cent done. Add the courgettes and cook lightly. Remove and set aside.

5. Discard the oil from the wok and sauté the Japanese leek and ginger until fragrant. Add the sauce and mix well. Return the squid and courgettes to the wok.

6. Add the palm oil and give it a quick stir. Arrange on a serving plate and serve.

Blanch the oysters in a pot of lightly salted water.

Drain the oysters and pat dry with paper towels.

Deep-fry the oysters until golden.

宫
保
牡
蛎

Kung Pao Oyster

SERVES	3–4
PREPARATION TIME	20 minutes
COOKING TIME	10 minutes

S zechwan *kung pao* chicken is a dish known for its complex combination of sweet, salty, sour, and spicy flavours. Instead of chicken, I use oysters in this rendition, ideally the meatier variety like Pacific oysters. When frying the oysters, you want to achieve a crisp outer layer while retaining a juicy centre.

INGREDIENTS

5–8	oysters
1 tsp	salt
As needed	potato starch
15	gingko nuts, shelled
5	facing heaven peppers, halved
5–8	red Szechwan peppercorns
1 tsp	grated garlic
15 g	Japanese leek, white part, sliced
15 g	red capsicum, cut into small squares

SAUCE

1½ Tbsp	sugar
1 Tbsp	Japanese rice vinegar
1 Tbsp	Shaoxing rice wine
½ Tbsp	Zhenjiang vinegar
½ Tbsp	Chinese fermented rice (*jiuniang*)
½ Tbsp	Japanese soy sauce
1½ Tbsp	potato starch, mixed with a little water into a paste
1 Tbsp	chicken stock (page 139)

METHOD

1. Remove the oysters from their shells and rinse with lightly salted water and some potato starch.

2. Blanch the oysters in a pot of lightly salted water. Remove and pat dry. Coat with potato starch.

3. Heat sufficient oil for deep-frying in a wok to 200°C and deep-fry the oysters until golden. Remove and set aside.

4. Add the gingko nuts and deep-fry until golden. Remove and peel off the thin skin. Set aside.

5. Drain the oil from the wok and sauté the facing heaven peppers, peppercorns, grated garlic, Japanese leek, and capsicum over low heat until fragrant.

6. Return the oysters and gingko nuts to the wok. Mix well.

7. Add the ingredients for the sauce and sauté lightly. Arrange on a serving plate and serve.

Sautéed Shrimp with Mala Mayonnaise

麻辣蛋黄酱明虾

SERVES 4
PREPARATION TIME 30 minutes
COOKING TIME 10 minutes

Adding *mala* flavours to the original recipe is my own take on this popular dish. It showcases just how versatile Szechwan spices can be.

INGREDIENTS

4	black tiger shrimps, about 150 g in total
1 pinch	salt
½ Tbsp	sake
½ Tbsp	egg white
½ Tbsp	potato starch
As needed	cooking oil
40 g	green courgette, cut into bite-sized pieces
40 g	*eryngii* mushrooms, cut into bite-sized pieces

MALA BASE

100 g	fried shallots
5 g	fried garlic
360 ml	Japanese soy sauce
240 g	sugar
60 ml	cooking oil
20 g	chilli powder
50 ml	Japanese rice vinegar

MALA MAYONNAISE

| 100 g | *mala* base |
| 150 g | mayonnaise |

METHOD

1. Prepare the *mala* base for the *mala* mayonnaise.

2. Finely chop the fried shallots and fried garlic using a food processor. Place in a pot with the soy sauce and sugar. Bring to a boil, then set aside to cool.

3. Heat the oil in a wok and sauté the chilli powder. Add this to the cooled fried shallots and fried garlic mixture in step 2. Set aside to cool.

4. When the mixture is cool, add the vinegar.

5. Measure out 100 g of the *mala* base sauce and mix it with the mayonnaise to make *mala* mayonnaise. The excess *mala* base can be kept in an airtight container and stored in the refrigerator for up to 2 weeks.

6. Peel the shrimps and cut into bite-sized pieces. Season with salt, sake, egg white, and potato starch.

7. Heat some oil in a wok and deep-fry the shrimps until golden. Drain and set aside.

8. In a clean wok, sauté the courgette and mushrooms lightly. Add the shrimps and mix well. Lower the heat and add the *mala* mayonnaise. Mix well.

9. Arrange on a serving plate and serve.

INGREDIENTS

500 g	spare ribs
2–3 stalks	Japanese leek, green part
3–4 slices	ginger, peeled
30–50 g	potato starch
As needed	cooking oil
4	large shrimps, trimmed and cut along the back
60 g	potatoes, cut into rectangular slices
60 g	lotus root, cut into rectangular slices
60 g	cucumber, cut into rectangular slices
15 g	facing heaven peppers
5 g	green Szechwan peppercorns
5 g	red Szechwan peppercorns
2 Tbsp	*lao you*
60 g	shallots, peeled and cut into small pieces

Dry-fried Shrimp and Spare Rib

干炒香辣排骨虾

SERVES	4
PREPARATION TIME	20 minutes + overnight marination
COOKING TIME	1½ hours

20 g	garlic, peeled and thinly sliced
20 g	ginger, peeled and thinly sliced
1	green chilli, sliced
1	red chilli, sliced
1 Tbsp	chilli bean paste (*doubanjiang*)
1 Tbsp	Shaoxing rice wine
1 tsp	sugar
½ Tbsp	chicken seasoning powder
1 tsp	cumin
1 tsp	Chinese five-spice powder
1 Tbsp	toasted white sesame seeds
2–3 sprigs	coriander leaves

MARINADE

½ Tbsp	fermented black beans (*douchi*)
½ tsp	grated garlic
2 Tbsp	Shaoxing rice wine
2 Tbsp	oyster sauce
1 tsp	Japanese soy sauce
1 pinch	salt

A popular trend that has caught on in China is the *mala* dry-fry as showcased in this recipe. The hodgepodge of meats, seafood, and vegetables can be easily adjusted to serve any number of guests, making it a great party dish.

METHOD

1. Prepare the ribs a day ahead. Cut the ribs along the bone and wash with running water for 5 minutes. Pat dry and rub in the marinade. Place in the refrigerator to marinate overnight.

2. Place the ribs in a steamer with the Japanese leek and ginger, and steam for 1 hour. Coat the ribs in potato starch.

3. Heat 1 litre oil in a wok over high heat. Add the ribs and deep-fry for 2–3 minutes. Add the shrimps, potatoes, lotus root, and cucumber. Deep-fry until the shrimps change colour and are done. Remove and set aside.

4. Heat some oil in a clean wok and sauté the facing heaven peppers, peppercorns, *lao you*, shallots, garlic, ginger, and chillies until fragrant.

5. Add the ribs and shrimp mixture, followed by the chilli bean paste. Mix well.

6. Add the rice wine, sugar, chicken seasoning powder, cumin, and five-spice powder. Sauté to mix.

7. Transfer to a serving dish. Garnish with sesame seeds and coriander leaves. Serve.

SERVES	4
PREPARATION TIME	10 minutes
COOKING TIME	20 minutes

Braised Three Treasures in Soy Sauce

红烧三宝

INGREDIENTS

4	chicken wings
1 tsp	Shaoxing rice wine
1 tsp	Japanese soy sauce
1	Japanese leek, white part
As needed	cooking oil
40 g	dried shiitake mushrooms, soaked to rehydrate and cut into 1-cm slices
60 g	lotus root, cut into 5-mm slices
1 Tbsp	shallot oil
500 ml	chicken stock (page 139)
300 ml	pork stock (page 139)
1	abalone, boiled
120 g	sea cucumber, soaked to rehydrate
3 Tbsp	potato starch, mixed with a little water into a paste
2 tsp	chicken oil (page 139)

SEASONING

1½ Tbsp	oyster sauce
1 Tbsp	Japanese soy sauce
1 dash	ground white pepper
1 tsp	light soy sauce
1 Tbsp	sugar

As the name suggests, this is an auspicious dish featuring premium ingredients traditionally simmered in soy sauce. Serving this dish during Chinese New Year is said to bring luck and prosperity.

METHOD

1. Cut the wing tips off the chicken wings and season with the rice wine and soy sauce.

2. Make diagonal slits on the Japanese leek, then cut into 5-cm lengths.

3. Heat some oil in a wok over high heat and deep-fry the chicken wings until the skin is crispy. Add the mushrooms and lotus root, and give it a quick stir. Remove and drain.

4. Heat shallot oil in another wok and sauté the Japanese leek until fragrant.

5. Add both the stocks, chicken wings, mushrooms, lotus root, abalone, and sea cucumbers. Bring to a boil, then lower the heat and simmer for about 10 minutes.

6. Add the seasoning and simmer for a few minutes to allow the flavours to blend. Add the potato starch paste to thicken the sauce. Drizzle with chicken oil and serve.

Noodles & Rice

面条与米饭

Sauté the minced pork until the liquid that emerges from the meat is clear.

Add the rice wine, soy sauce, and sweet bean paste, and sauté until the flavours blend.

Dan Dan Noodle Soup 担担面

SERVES 1
PREPARATION TIME 10 minutes
COOKING TIME 20 minutes

INGREDIENTS

5 g	Szechwan preserved mustard greens (*ya cai*)
20 g	Japanese leek, white part, chopped
1 tsp	lard
½ tsp	Japanese rice vinegar
2 Tbsp	Japanese soy sauce
1 Tbsp	Chinese sesame paste
1 Tbsp	chilli oil
80 g	fresh Chinese egg noodles
2–3 stalks	green vegetables
300 ml	chicken stock (page 139)

ZHAJIANG SAUCE

1 Tbsp	cooking oil
300 g	minced pork
2 Tbsp	Shaoxing rice wine
1 Tbsp	Japanese soy sauce
1 Tbsp	sweet bean paste (*tianmianjiang*)

Dan dan noodles were traditionally served dry by street vendors in the Szechwan province. My grandfather came up with this recipe after my grandmother advised him that the Japanese preferred to have their noodles with soup.

METHOD

1. Prepare the *zhajiang* sauce. Heat the oil in a wok over medium heat. Add the minced pork and sauté until the liquid that emerges from the meat is clear.

2. Add the rice wine, soy sauce, and sweet bean paste. Sauté until the flavours blend. Set 1–2 Tbsp *zhajiang* sauce aside as a topping for the noodles. Any excess *zhajiang* sauce can be kept in an airtight container in the refrigerator for up to 10 days.

3. Place the Szechwan preserved mustard greens, Japanese leek, lard, rice vinegar, soy sauce, sesame paste, and chilli oil in a serving bowl.

4. Boil a pot of water and lightly cook the noodles. Drain and place in the bowl.

5. Boil the green vegetables and drain well. Set aside.

6. Bring the chicken stock to a boil and ladle over the noodles. Add some *zhajiang* sauce and the green vegetables. Serve.

Yibin-style Noodle with Pickled Vegetable

宜宾燃面

SERVES	2
PREPARATION TIME	10 minutes
COOKING TIME	10 minutes

This dish is a specialty of Yibin prefecture in the southeastern part of the Szechwan province, the home town of my grandfather.

INGREDIENTS

½ Tbsp	cooking oil
160 g	minced pork
1 Tbsp	Shaoxing rice wine
½ Tbsp	Japanese soy sauce
½ Tbsp	sweet bean paste (*tianmianjiang*)
160 g	fresh Chinese egg noodles
25 g	Szechwan preserved mustard greens, minced
1	spring onion, chopped
50 g	Japanese leek, white part, chopped
30 g	peanuts, crushed
1 tsp	chilli powder

SEASONING

1½ Tbsp	Japanese soy sauce
⅔ Tbsp	sweet bean paste (*tianmianjiang*)
⅔ Tbsp	sesame oil
1 pinch	salt
1 Tbsp	chicken stock (page 139)

METHOD

1. Heat the oil in a wok over medium heat. Add the minced pork and sauté until the liquid that emerges from the meat is clear.

2. Add the rice wine, soy sauce, and sweet bean paste, and sauté until the meat has absorbed the sauces. Dish out and set aside.

3. Boil a pot of water and lightly cook the noodles. Drain and divide equally between two serving bowls.

4. Combine the ingredients for the seasoning and pour it over the noodles. Mix the noodles lightly with the seasoning.

5. Top the noodles with the Szechwan preserved mustard greens, spring onion, Japanese leek, peanuts, minced meat, and chilli powder. Serve.

SERVES	1
PREPARATION TIME	10 minutes
COOKING TIME	1 hour

Bang Bang Chicken Noodle

凉拌棒棒鸡面

INGREDIENTS

1	spring chicken
2-cm knob	ginger, peeled and sliced
1	Japanese leek, green part
80 g	fresh Chinese egg noodles
1 pinch	salt
½ tsp	sesame oil
1	tomato, sliced
1	Japanese cucumber, peeled and sliced
1	green shiso leaf

BANG BANG CHICKEN SAUCE

6 Tbsp	sugar
3 Tbsp	Japanese rice vinegar
1 Tbsp	grated ginger
195 ml	Japanese soy sauce
6 Tbsp	Chinese sesame paste
2 Tbsp	chilli oil
1	spring onion, chopped
2 Tbsp	sesame oil

Bang bang chicken got its name from the manner of using a mallet to tenderise the chicken. My grandfather took inspiration from the Japanese cold ramen, *hiyashi chūka*, for this recipe.

METHOD

1. Boil the chicken in an ample amount of water with the ginger and Japanese leek for 30–40 minutes. Clear juice should emerge when the thickest parts of the chicken is pricked.

2. Drain the chicken thoroughly and pat dry. Shred the meat finely and set aside. There will be enough meat for 8 portions. Keep the excess in an airtight container and store refrigerated for up to 2 days.

3. Boil a pot of water and lightly cook the noodles. Drain and place in a serving bowl. Add the salt and sesame oil. Toss to mix, then leave the noodles to cool until room temperature.

4. Combine all the ingredients for the *bang bang* chicken sauce. Set 2–3 Tbsp of the sauce aside as a topping for the noodles. Any excess sauce can be kept in an airtight container in the refrigerator for up to 10 days.

5. Arrange the noodles, chicken, tomato, cucumber, and green shiso leaf on a serving plate. Top with the *bang bang* chicken sauce and serve.

SERVES	3–4
PREPARATION TIME	5 minutes
COOKING TIME	5 minutes

Chengdu-style Chilli Noodle

成都甜水面

INGREDIENTS

500 g	udon
2 Tbsp	sesame oil
1 dash	chilli oil
3 g	toasted white sesame seeds
1 tsp	grated garlic

SAUCE

100 ml	sweet soy sauce (*tianjiangyou*)
30 g	grated garlic
80 ml	chilli oil
1 tsp	paste from chilli oil

This unique vegetarian thick noodle dish has long been popular in restaurants in the Szechwan province. When my grandfather first served it in Japan, he improvised by replacing the noodles with the locally available udon, a type of thick wheat flour noodle. The sesame oil and sweet soy sauce give the dish a sweet fragrant aroma, while the grated garlic adds zing.

METHOD

1. Combine all the ingredients for the sauce and set aside.

2. Boil a pot of water and lightly cook the udon. Drain and transfer the udon to a mixing bowl. Drizzle with sesame oil and mix well to prevent the udon from sticking.

3. Divide the udon equally among 3–4 serving bowls. Cover with sauce.

4. Top with more chilli oil, sesame seeds, and grated garlic. Serve.

SERVES	2
PREPARATION TIME	10 minutes
COOKING TIME	20 minutes

Fried Rice with Crabmeat Sauce

蟹肉烩炒饭

INGREDIENTS

2 Tbsp	shallot oil
3 Tbsp	beaten egg
150 g	frozen cooked rice, thawed
1 pinch	salt
1 dash	ground white pepper
1 tsp	sake
2 Tbsp	chopped Japanese leek, white part

CRABMEAT SAUCE

2 Tbsp	shallot oil
50 g	crab claw meat, boiled
40 g	boiled bamboo shoot, cut into small pieces
2–3 spears	green asparagus, cut into small pieces
200 ml	chicken stock (page 139)
1 Tbsp	sake
½ tsp	salt
1 pinch	sugar
1 dash	ground white pepper
2 Tbsp	potato starch, mixed with a little water into a paste
2 Tbsp	egg white
1 tsp	evaporated milk
1 Tbsp	chicken oil (page 139)

Deliciously filling, the savoury pairing of the fried rice and crabmeat makes this an ideal comfort food.

METHOD

1. Prepare the crabmeat sauce. Heat the shallot oil in a wok and lightly sauté the crab claw meat, bamboo shoot, and asparagus.

2. Add the chicken stock, sake, salt, sugar, and pepper, and bring to a boil. Lower the heat to a simmer, then add the potato starch paste to thicken the sauce.

3. Stir the egg white into the evaporated milk and add the mixture to the wok. Add the chicken oil. Set the crabmeat sauce aside.

4. Heat the shallot oil in another wok and add the beaten egg. Add the thawed rice, salt, pepper, and sake, and mix well. Add the Japanese leek and mix again.

5. Transfer the fried rice to a serving dish. Top with the crabmeat sauce and serve.

Peel the eggplants to create an alternating pattern.

Roll-cut the peeled eggplants to get bite-sized pieces.

Arrange the cooked rice and ingredients in a well-heated stone bowl.

Bibimbap-style Yuxiang Eggplant

石锅鱼香茄子饭

SERVES	2
PREPARATION TIME	10 minutes
COOKING TIME	20 minutes

INGREDIENTS

40 g	carrot, shredded
60 g	soy bean sprouts
1 pinch	salt
½ tsp	sesame oil
3–4	Japanese eggplants
2–3 Tbsp	cornstarch
As needed	cooking oil
100 g	minced pork
50 g	Japanese leek, white part, chopped
2–3 Tbsp	potato starch, mixed with a little water into a paste
½ tsp	Japanese rice vinegar
200 g	cooked rice
60 g	lettuce, finely sliced
1 strip	dried seaweed, finely sliced

SAUCE

2 tsp	grated ginger
1 tsp	grated garlic
½ Tbsp	Chinese fermented rice (*jiuniang*)
1 Tbsp	chilli bean paste (*doubanjiang*)
1 Tbsp	sweet bean paste (*tianmianjiang*)

SEASONING

200 ml	chicken stock (page 139)
½ Tbsp	Shaoxing rice wine
1 Tbsp	Japanese soy sauce
1½ Tbsp	sugar
1 dash	ground white pepper

Here I use a Szechwan sauce mixture known as *yuxiang*—commonly made with ingredients like ginger, garlic, sugar, vinegar, and chilli peppers. I arrange the ingredients in the style of a Korean bibimbap and serve it in a heated stone bowl, as I find that this elevates the flavours and appearance of the dish.

METHOD

1. Lightly boil the carrot and soy bean sprouts. Pat dry and season with salt and sesame oil. Set aside.

2. To enhance the taste of the eggplants, cut the stalk and peel the skin to create an alternating pattern. Roll-cut the eggplants to get bite-sized pieces.
   Lightly wet the eggplants with some water, then coat with cornstarch.

3. Heat sufficient oil for deep-frying in a wok to 180°C and deep-fry the eggplants until crisp on the outside. Remove and set aside.

4. Drain the oil from the wok. Add the minced pork and sauté. Combine the ingredients for the sauce and add to the wok.

5. Combine the ingredients for the seasoning and add to the wok. Add the fried eggplants and simmer for 1–2 minutes for the flavours to blend.

6. Add the Japanese leek, then stir in the potato starch paste to thicken the sauce. Add the rice vinegar.

7. Arrange the cooked rice, lettuce, carrot, soy bean sprouts, and seaweed in a well-heated stone bowl, then top with the cooked eggplant and meat mixture. Serve.

1

Flatten the squid tube using the flat side of a chopper.

2

Score the squid with criss-cross cuts.

3

Cut the squid into bite-sized pieces.

4

Deep-fry the scorched rice until puffed and golden.

SERVES	34
PREPARATION TIME	20 minutes
COOKING TIME	15 minutes

什锦柚子酱锅巴

Scorched Rice with Seafood, Pork, and Assorted Vegetables in Yuzu Sauce

INGREDIENTS

40 g	squid tube
50 g	pork (hind leg)
40 g	shrimps
1 Tbsp	Shaoxing rice wine
¼ tsp	salt
1 dash	ground white pepper
2–3 Tbsp	potato starch, mixed with a little water into a paste
As needed	cooking oil
40 g	boiled bamboo shoot, finely sliced
2	dried shiitake mushrooms, soaked to rehydrate, finely sliced
1 slice	ham, sliced
30 g	crabmeat
8 pieces	scorched rice (*guoba*)

YUZU SAUCE

700 ml	chicken stock (page 139)
1 Tbsp	sake
2 Tbsp	Japanese soy sauce
1 pinch	salt
1 dash	ground white pepper
1½ Tbsp	sugar
2 Tbsp	potato starch, mixed with a little water into a paste
1 Tbsp	Japanese rice vinegar
5 g	grated yuzu peel

The crusty remnants formed on the bottom of a pot when cooking rice, scorched rice is commonly eaten as a snack in China. When deep-fried, it becomes a crispy rice cracker. Widely popular in Szechwan cuisine, scorched rice is often served with thick sauces and stews.

METHOD

1. Cut the squid tube open and flatten using the flat side of a chopper. Score with criss-cross cuts, then slice it lengthwise in half. Cut into bite-sized pieces.

2. Score the pork and cut into bite-sized pieces. Peel the shrimps and make a cut down the back of each shrimp.

3. Place the squid, pork, and shrimps in a bowl and season with the rice wine, salt, pepper, and potato starch paste.

4. Heat some oil in a wok and lightly sauté the squid, pork, and shrimps. Remove and set aside.

5. In a deep pan, add the bamboo shoot, mushrooms, ham, and the ingredients for the yuzu sauce, except for the potato starch paste, rice vinegar, and yuzu peel. Bring to a boil, then stir in the crabmeat and cooked squid, pork, and shrimps.

6. Add the potato starch paste and simmer to thicken the sauce. Add the vinegar and yuzu peel.

7. Heat sufficient oil for deep-frying in a wok to 180°C and deep-fry the scorched rice until puffed and golden. Drain well and arrange in a serving bowl.

8. Ladle the yuzu sauce over the scorched rice and serve.

什锦柚子酱锅巴

Desserts 甜点

Almond Pudding with White Fungus

银耳杏仁豆腐

SERVES	4
PREPARATION TIME	10 minutes + 2 hours setting time
COOKING TIME	10 minutes

INGREDIENTS

1 handful	white fungus, soaked to rehydrate
700 ml	water
5–6 g	agar strips, soaked to rehydrate and sliced
3 Tbsp	almond powder
40 g	sugar
50 ml	evaporated milk
50 ml	milk
1 slice	honeydew
1 handful	goji berries, soaked to rehydrate

SYRUP

200 ml	water
40 g	sugar

METHOD

1. Prepare the syrup. Bring the water to a boil and add the sugar. Stir until the sugar is melted. Set aside to cool, then refrigerate to chill.

2. Prepare the white fungus. Boil some water in a pot and add a little sugar (in addition to the amounts listed). Add the white fungus and simmer for 2 minutes. Set aside.

3. Bring the 700 ml water to a boil and add the agar strips, almond powder, and sugar. Simmer over low heat until the agar strips are completely dissolved. Turn off the heat and stir in the evaporated milk and milk.

4. Strain the almond mixture and pour into a mould. Leave to set.

5. Cut the set almond agar into 1.5-cm pieces. Cut the honeydew to the same size. Place in a serving bowl.

6. Add the white fungus and goji berries. Ladle the syrup over and serve.

Mango Pudding

芒果布丁

SERVES	4
PREPARATION TIME	10 minutes + 2 hours setting time
COOKING TIME	10 minutes

INGREDIENTS

200 g	ripe mangoes
3 g	gelatin powder
50 ml	hot water
20 g	sugar
25 g	crushed ice
25 ml	heavy cream

GARNISHING

A few	ripe mango cubes
2–3 sprigs	mint leaves

METHOD

1. Peel the mangoes and slice the flesh. Place in a bowl and mash lightly.

2. Place the gelatin powder in a bowl. Add the hot water and stir until the gelatin is completely dissolved. If the gelatin does not dissolve easily, try heating in a microwave oven or placing the mixture on the stove.

3. Add the sugar and stir until the sugar is dissolved.

4. Add the crushed ice and mix.

5. Add the mashed mangoes and heavy cream. Mix well.

6. Pour the mixture into a bowl and place in the refrigerator to set.

7. Top the set pudding with mango cubes and mint leaves. Serve.

Add the coconut milk to the batter and mix well.

Add the egg mixture to the boiling water while stirring constantly.

Stir until the mixture thickens into a paste.

Pour the paste into an well-oiled tray to set.

Deep-fried Custard 油炸奶黄

SERVES	4
PREPARATION TIME	10 minutes + 2–3 hours setting time
COOKING TIME	25 minutes

INGREDIENTS

330 ml	water
As needed	sesame oil
As needed	cooking oil
30 g	Japanese roasted soybean flour (*kinako*), for dusting

EGG MIXTURE

20 g	potato starch
80 g	plain flour
40 g	sugar
5	beaten eggs
200 ml	coconut milk

METHOD

1. Bring the water to a boil.

2. Prepare the egg mixture. Mix the potato starch, plain flour, and sugar in a bowl. Add the beaten eggs a little at a time, stirring with a whisk, until the mixture is smooth.

3. Add the coconut milk and mix well.

4. Add the egg mixture to the boiling water, a little at a time, stirring constantly until the mixture thickens into a paste.

5. Coat a tray well with sesame oil and pour the paste into the tray. Level with the back of an oiled spoon.

6. Refrigerate the custard for 2–3 hours until set.

7. Cut the custard into rectangular pieces.

8. Heat sufficient oil for deep-frying in a wok and deep-fry the pieces of custard until golden. Drain well.

9. Coat the pieces of custard with soybean flour and arrange on a serving plate. Serve.

基本食譜

Basic Recipes

Chicken Stock

鸡
上
汤

INGREDIENTS

1	stewing chicken
200 g	chicken feet
50 g	ginger, peeled and sliced
10 g	Japanese leek, green part
2 litres	water

METHOD

1. Wash the chicken and chicken feet.

2. Boil a large pot of water and blanch the chicken and chicken feet. Remove and rinse.

3. Place the chicken and chicken feet into a clean pot with the ginger and Japanese leek. Bring to a boil, then simmer for 1 hour over low heat.

4. Strain the stock. Use as needed.

Pork Stock

猪
上
汤

INGREDIENTS

1	stewing chicken
200 g	chicken feet
500 g	pork bones
100 g	pork fat
50 g	ginger, peeled and sliced
10 g	Japanese leek, green part
3 litres	water

METHOD

1. Wash the chicken and chicken feet.

2. Boil a large pot of water and blanch the chicken, chicken feet, and pork bones. Remove and rinse.

3. Place all the ingredients in a clean pot and boil over high heat for 2 hours, adding more water as necessary.

4. Strain the stock. Use as needed.

Chicken Oil

鸡
油

INGREDIENTS

2 kg	chicken fat
10 g	ginger, peeled and sliced
50 g	Japanese leek, green part

METHOD

1. Combine the chicken fat, ginger, and Japanese leek in a heatproof bowl. Place in a steamer and steam for 3 hours.

2. Skim off the top layer of oil for use as needed. Discard the other ingredients.

食
材

Glossary

Fresh Ingredients

Bamboo shoot
This tender, young shoot of the bamboo plant has a crunchy texture and mild, sweet flavour. While it is available fresh, vacuum-sealed or canned, vacuum-sealed bamboo shoot is a convenient option, being already cleaned and precooked. Rinse well before use.

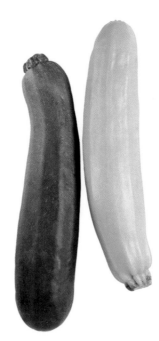

Courgette
Also known as zucchini, the courgette is part of the squash family. The most common variety is dark green in colour, but there is also a yellow variety that I like to use to add colour to dishes. Select firm, heavy fruit with shiny, blemish-free skin.

Daikon
The daikon resembles a carrot and is known as white carrot or white radish in Chinese. A member of the radish family, the daikon has a crisp texture and earthy flavour when raw, and becomes sweet and meltingly tender when cooked. Select roots that are firm with smooth, cream-coloured skin.

Japanese cucumber
This long and slender variety of cucumber has dark green skin and very fine seeds. It is crisp and succulent, making it ideal for use in salads and tossed dishes. I used Japanese cucumber in the recipes in this book, but English cucumbers can be used as well.

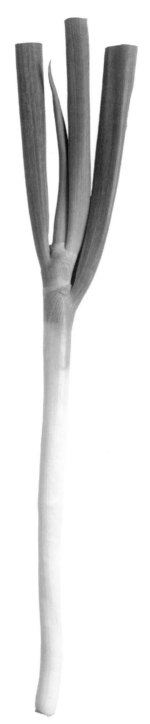

Japanese eggplant
Japanese eggplant is long and slender with thin, deep purple skin and tender, cream-coloured flesh. When cooked, the flesh becomes soft and creamy, and simply steaming them brings out their sweetness. Select fruit that feel heavy and firm, with no soft or brown spots.

Japanese leek
There are many varieties of leek, and this is the most common variety used in Japanese cooking. The white part has a mild and sweet flavour and is used as an ingredient in dishes, while the green top is added when blanching to remove impurities from meat and poultry.

Japanese spring onion
Japanese spring onion is larger than regular spring onion, and has a more robust flavour. I add it to braised or stir-fried dishes for a touch of sweetness.

Lotus root

This underwater rhizome of the lotus plant is
recognisable by its segments that are connected
like a chain. When sliced in rounds, it reveals
a pretty pattern created by its holes. Lotus root
is a versatile ingredient that I use to add bite
and sweetness to dishes. Select roots that are
firm with no soft or brown spots. Scrub well
and trim the ends before use.

Shishito peppers

These small finger-length peppers are green
in colour with slightly wrinkly skin. They are
mildly hot and can be used to add a sweet
and spicy flavour to dishes.

Spring onion

The spring onion is from the same family
as leek and has a flavour similar to leek.
It is used mostly as a garnish to finish a dish,
but can also be used for braises and stir-fries
for added flavour.

Mushrooms

Enoki
Also known as *enokitake* or golden needle mushrooms, these delicate mushrooms with long and thin white stalks, and small white caps are sold in bunches with their woody end intact. Trim this off and rinse well before use. Enoki mushrooms are mild in flavour and are enjoyed for their crunchy texture.

Eryngii
Also known as king oyster or king trumpet mushroom, the *eryngii* mushroom has a thick stem and small, flat cap. When cooked, the mushroom remains firm with a meaty texture.

Maitake
The *maitake* mushroom is also known as Hen of the Woods. It grows in overlapping layers with fan-shaped caps. It has an intense, woody flavour and delicate texture.

Shiitake
A popular mushroom, the shiitake is also commonly available dried. I use both fresh and dried shiitake mushrooms in my cooking for their deep and meaty flavour.

Dried and Preserved Ingredients

Century egg
This is egg cured in a mixture of salt, lime and ash. The yolk is greenish grey and creamy, and the white is jelly-like, translucent and dark brown. It has a strong flavour and goes well in salads and stir-fries.

Dried sea cucumber
Dried sea cucumber requires soaking before it can be added to the pot. The rehydrating process takes about a week. As a first step, soak the sea cucumber in hot water until the water turns cool, then drain and repeat this step. When the water turns cool for the second time, drain the sea cucumber, then place in ice-cold water and leave to sit in the fridge overnight. Repeat these steps for about a week until the sea cucumber has a soft texture. Rehydrated sea cucumber is available, but check that there is no fishy odour before buying.

Dried scallop
Also known as conpoy, dried scallop is appreciated for its sweet, umami flavour that adds depth to sauces, soups, and stocks.

Facing heaven pepper
A staple of the Szechwan kitchen, this cone-shaped pepper is also known as *chao tian jiao*. It is a medium-hot pepper with a citrus note. Stir-frying helps bring out its flavour.

Five-spice powder

The sweet and aromatic five-spice powder is made up of a blend of spices that usually includes cloves, cinnamon, fennel seeds, star anise, and Szechwan pepper. It can be used to marinate meat and poultry, or added as a seasoning when cooking.

Gingko nuts

These oval-shaped nuts of the gingko tree are typically sold dried, shelled in vacuum-sealed packs, or canned. To prepare the dried nuts, shell, then boil and remove the membrane. Gingko nuts have a mild flavour and are soft and chewy. They can be used in both sweet and savoury preparations.

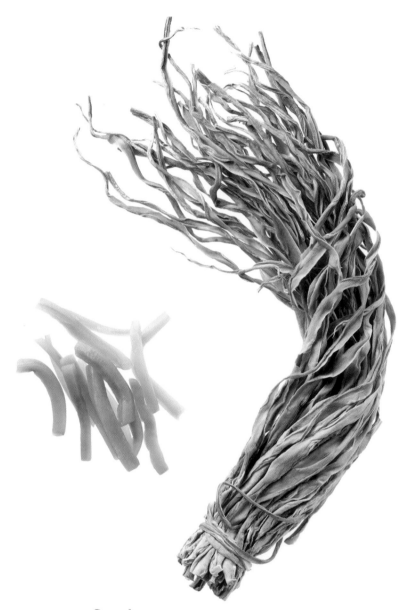

Gong choy

Also known as *yamakurage* and mountain jelly vegetable, *gong choy* is available dried (*pictured right*) or reconstituted (*pictured left*). *Gong choy* is enjoyed for its crisp texture and is popularly used in salads and stir-fries. If unavailable, substitute with like-textured vegetables such as stem lettuce and asparagus.

Hawk claw chillies
Known in Japan as *takanotsume* peppers, hawk
claw chillies are so named because they are
curved and shaped like talons. These chillies
are fiery hot, so use according to taste. Wear
rubber gloves when handling chillies to avoid
leaving a burning sensation on your skin.

**Szechwan preserved mustard greens
(ya cai)**
Another key ingredient in Szechwan cuisine,
Szechwan preserved mustard greens is made
by pickling the leaves of mustard greens with
salt and spices. It is available in small packets
from Chinese supermarkets.

Szechwan peppercorns, green and red
One of the key ingredients in Szechwan cuisine,
Szechwan peppercorns add fragrance to dishes,
but can also cause a mouth-numbing sensation
if bitten into. Red peppercorns have a more
intense numbing effect, while green peppercorns
are more fragrant. Whole peppercorns (*pictured
left*) are typically used to infuse oils for cooking,
while the powdered versions (*pictured right*) are
added directly to season dishes.

Oils, Sauces and Vinegars

Chilli bean paste (*doubanjiang*)
This savoury paste is an essential ingredient used in preparing many of the Szechwan dishes featured in this book. It is made by fermenting broad beans with chillies. When cooked, it imparts a deep and complex umami flavour to dishes. There are many varieties of chilli bean paste available. For Szechwan cooking, choose Szechwan chilli bean paste.

Chinese sesame paste
Made from roasted sesame seeds, Chinese sesame paste has a strong nutty aroma and is typically used in Chinese cuisine to flavour sauces for noodle dishes and salads.

Japanese soy sauce
When using soy sauce as a seasoning, I typically use Japanese soy sauce or *shoyu* for its rich aroma and flavour. Chinese soy sauce can be used in place of Japanese soy sauce, but the flavour will be different.

Chilli oil
This deep red-coloured oil is derived from infusing chillies in oil. Bottled chilli oil purchased from the supermarket may include chilli flakes. Chilli oil can be used as a seasoning when cooking and it can also be drizzled over cooked dishes as a final flourish to the dish.

Fermented black beans (*douchi*)
Made by fermenting soy beans in a mixture of water, salt and sugar, these black beans pack a punch of flavour and are commonly used in Chinese stir-fries or steamed dishes. Fermented black beans is an essential ingredient in my *mapo* tofu dish.

Lao you
Lao you is commonly used in Szechwan cooking. Like chilli oil, it is made by infusing various spices such as Szechwan peppercorns, garlic and ginger in oil. I use it to add depth of flavour to dishes.

Chinese fermented rice (*jiuniang*)
Variously known as *lao zao*, Chinese rice sauce or Chinese rice pudding, Chinese fermented rice is made by fermenting cooked glutinous rice with a yeast starter. It is popularly used in Chinese desserts and Szechwan cooking to add flavour and a touch of sweetness.

Japanese rice vinegar
This pale yellow vinegar is seasoned with sake, sugar and salt to give it a light and delicate flavour. It is most commonly used as a seasoning for sushi rice, and can also be used in sauces, marinades, and dressings for an additional depth of flavour.

Oyster sauce
A popular seasoning used in Chinese stir-fries, this thick, savoury sauce is made by caramelising oyster juices. It has a rich, briny flavour that goes well with a wide range of ingredients, from meat and poultry, to vegetables and tofu.

Palm oil
Palm oil is a versatile cooking oil and it is rich in carotene. I use it to give dishes a lovely orange hue. It can be replaced with other cooking oils if you prefer not to use palm oil.

Sweet bean paste (*tianmianjiang*)
Sometimes also known as sweet flour sauce, this thick, brown sauce has a sweet and salty umami flavour. It is a pantry staple in Chinese cuisine and can be used as a seasoning and marinade, as well as a dipping sauce.

Vincotto
This is a cooked Italian wine similar to balsamic vinegar. Made from grapes, it is sweet and thick, with a fruity flavour. It can be used as a seasoning for meat, a salad dressing, and a topping on desserts.

Sesame oil
Extracted from sesame seeds, sesame oil has an appetising aromatic and nutty flavour. Unlike other cooking oils, sesame oil is not typically used for stir-frying or deep-frying. It is added at the end of cooking as a flavour enhancer, and tossed with ingredients as a sauce.

Sweet soy sauce (*tianjiangyou*)
This is basically soy sauce sweetened with palm sugar to give it a dark, syrupy consistency, and a sweet savoury note. It is used in stir-fries and braises, and it can also be added directly to season dishes.

Zhenjiang vinegar
Also known as Chinkiang vinegar or simply Chinese black vinegar, this vinegar is brewed from glutinous rice and wheat bran, and has a full-bodied and sweet flavour. It is an essential ingredient in Szechwan cuisine and is used in stir-frys, braises, and sauces.

Shaoxing rice wine
Shaoxing rice wine is made from fermented glutinous rice. This aromatic wine has a distinctive fragrance and it is used in Chinese cooking to enhance the flavour of dishes. There are many types of Shaoxing rice wine available and price is usually an indication of quality, so choose the best you can find.

Szechwan pepper oil
Infused with Szechwan peppercorns, Szechwan pepper oil adds an intense, tongue-numbing sensation to dishes it is added to. It is often used in sauces and dressing for an authentic *mala* flavour. A little goes a long way, so do a taste test before adding more to avoid drowning out the other flavours in the dish.

索引

Index of Recipes

Beef
Poached Sliced Beef in Hot Chilli Oil 81
Sautéed Beef with Cumin 85
Sliced Beef, Beef Tongue and Tripe with Mala Sauce 23
Steamed Beef with Toasted Rice Powder 79
Stir-fried Beef with Green Capsicum and Bamboo Shoot 65

Chicken
Bang Bang Chicken Noodle 117
Braised Three Treasures in Soy Sauce 109
Chicken Oil 139
Chicken Stock 139
Crispy Chilli Chicken 87
Daqian Chicken 83
Mixed Salad with Mala Dressing 21
Steamed Chicken Soup 45
Steamed Chicken with Mala Sauce 19
Szechwan-style Stewed Chicken in a Hot Stone Bowl 89

Desserts
Almond Pudding with White Fungus 133
Deep-fried Custard 137
Mango Pudding 135

Duck
Szechwan-style Tea-smoked Duck 69

Eggs
Capsicum and Century Egg with Fragrant Dressing 31
Deep-fried Custard 137
Foie Gras Chawanmushi with Crab Roe Soup 15
Fried Rice with Crabmeat Sauce 121
Mixed Salad with Mala Dressing 21
Steamed Eggplant with Shishito Pepper and Green Chilli Paste 27

Fish & Seafood
Ayu Spring Roll 33
Braised Three Treasures in Soy Sauce 109
Coral Trout Topped with Home-made Chilli Paste 99
Dry-fried Shrimp and Spare Rib 107
Foie Gras Chawanmushi with Crab Roe Soup 15
Fried Rice with Crabmeat Sauce 121
Kung Pao Oyster 103
Mixed Salad with Mala Dressing 21
Sautéed Shrimp with Mala Mayonnaise 105
Scorched Rice with Seafood, Pork, and Assorted Vegetables in Yuzu Sauce 127
Steamed Chicken Soup 45
Steamed Chinese Cabbage with Scallop 49
Stir-fried Lobster with Chilli Sauce 93
Stir-fried Squid with Cream Sauce 101
Szechwan Hot and Sour Soup 43
Turbot with Shishito Pepper 97

Mushrooms
Braised Three Treasures in Soy Sauce 109
Daqian Chicken 83
Sautéed Bok Choy and Duo Mushrooms with Black Truffle 53
Sautéed Shrimp with Mala Mayonnaise 105
Scorched Rice with Seafood, Pork, and Assorted Vegetables in Yuzu Sauce 127
Steamed Chicken Soup 45
Stir-fried Yuxiang Pork 75
Szechwan Hot and Sour Soup 43
Szechwan-style Stewed Chicken in a Hot Stone Bowl 89
Vegetarian Yuba-maki 25

Noodles
Bang Bang Chicken Noodle 117
Chengdu-style Chilli Noodle 119
Dan Dan Noodle Soup 113
Szechwan-style Stewed Chicken in a Hot Stone Bowl 89
Yibin-style Noodle with Pickled Vegetable 115

Pork
Bibimbap-style Yuxiang Eggplant 123
Boiled Szechwan Wonton with Spicy Sesame Sauce 37
Braised Tofu and Minced Pork with Chilli Bean Paste 55
Chen Family's Mapo Tofu 59
Chen Kenmin's Mapo Tofu 57
Dan Dan Noodle Soup 113
Dry-fried Shrimp and Spare Rib 107
Mixed Salad with Mala Dressing 21
Pork Belly and Daikon Soup 41
Pork Stock 139
Pork with Spicy Garlic Sauce 63
Sautéed Pork, Scallop, and Daikon Soup 47
Scorched Rice with Seafood, Pork, and Assorted Vegetables in Yuzu Sauce 127
Steamed Chinese Cabbage with Scallop 49
Steamed Pork Belly with Preserved Szechwan Mustard Greens 77
Stir-fried Yuxiang Pork 75
Sweet and Sour Pork with Black Vinegar 71
Szechwan Hot and Sour Soup 43
Twice-cooked Pork 67
Yibin-style Noodle with Pickled Vegetable 115

Rice
Bibimbap-style Yuxiang Eggplant 123
Fried Rice with Crabmeat Sauce 121
Scorched Rice with Seafood, Pork, and Assorted Vegetables in Yuzu Sauce 127
Steamed Beef with Toasted Rice Powder 79

Soups & Stews
Chengdu-style Vegetable Stew 51
Pork Belly and Daikon Soup 41
Sautéed Pork, Scallop, and Daikon Soup 47
Steamed Chicken Soup 45
Szechwan Hot and Sour Soup 43
Turbot with Shishito Pepper 97

Tofu
Braised Tofu and Minced Pork with Chilli Bean Paste 55
Chen Family's Mapo Tofu 59
Chen Kenmin's Mapo Tofu 57

Vegetables
Bibimbap-style Yuxiang Eggplant 123
Capsicum and Century Egg with Fragrant Dressing 31
Chengdu-style Vegetable Stew 51
Cold Steamed Chicken with Mala Sauce 19
Daqian Chicken 83
Mixed Salad with Mala Dressing 21
Sautéed Bok Choy and Duo Mushrooms with Black Truffle 53
Steamed Chinese Cabbage with Scallop 49
Steamed Eggplant with Shishito Pepper and Green Chilli Paste 27
Steamed Pork Belly with Preserved Szechwan Mustard Greens 77
Stir-fried Beef with Green Capsicum and Bamboo Shoot 65
Stir-fried Yuxiang Pork 75
Twice-cooked Pork 67
Vegetarian Yuba-maki 25
Yibin-style Noodle with Pickled Vegetable 115

Weights & Measures

Quantities for this book are given in metric and American spoon measures.

Standard spoon and cup measurements used are: 1 teaspoon = 5 ml, 1 tablespoon = 15 ml.

All measures are level unless otherwise stated.

LIQUID AND VOLUME MEASURES

Metric	Imperial	American
5 ml	⅙ fl oz	1 teaspoon
10 ml	⅓ fl oz	1 dessertspoon
15 ml	½ fl oz	1 tablespoon
60 ml	2 fl oz	¼ cup (4 tablespoons)
85 ml	2½ fl oz	⅛ cup
90 ml	3 fl oz	⅜ cup (6 tablespoons)
125 ml	4 fl oz	½ cup
180 ml	6 fl oz	¾ cup
250 ml	8 fl oz	1 cup
300 ml	10 fl oz (½ pint)	1¼ cups
375 ml	12 fl oz	1½ cups
435 ml	14 fl oz	1¾ cups
500 ml	16 fl oz	2 cups
625 ml	20 fl oz (1 pint)	2½ cups
750 ml	24 fl oz (1⅕ pints)	3 cups
1 litre	32 fl oz (1⅗ pints)	4 cups
1.25 litres	40 fl oz (2 pints)	5 cups
1.5 litres	48 fl oz (2⅖ pints)	6 cups
2.5 litres	80 fl oz (4 pints)	10 cups

DRY MEASURES

Metric	Imperial
30 grams	1 ounce
45 grams	1½ ounces
55 grams	2 ounces
70 grams	2½ ounces
85 grams	3 ounces
100 grams	3½ ounces
110 grams	4 ounces
125 grams	4½ ounces
140 grams	5 ounces
280 grams	10 ounces
450 grams	16 ounces (1 pound)
500 grams	1 pound, 1½ ounces
700 grams	1½ pounds
800 grams	1¾ pounds
1 kilogram	2 pounds, 3 ounces
1.5 kilograms	3 pounds, 4½ ounces
2 kilograms	4 pounds, 6 ounces

OVEN TEMPERATURE

	°C	°F	Gas Regulo
Very slow	120	250	1
Slow	150	300	2
Moderately slow	160	325	3
Moderate	180	350	4
Moderately hot	190/200	370/400	5/6
Hot	210/220	410/440	6/7
Very hot	230	450	8
Super hot	250/290	475/550	9/10

LENGTH

Metric	Imperial
0.5 cm	¼ inch
1 cm	½ inch
1.5 cm	¾ inch
2.5 cm	1 inch

ABBREVIATION

tsp	teaspoon
Tbsp	tablespoon
g	gram
kg	kilogram
ml	millilitre